HOW CAN I CAPITALIZE ON SOCIAL MEDIA WHEN MY KID HAS TO PROGRAM MY DVR?

THE BUSY EXECUTIVE'S GUIDE TO THE NEW TOOLS FOR BUILDING EVERY BUSINESS

Dave Nelsen has a unique ability to tackle an issue and distill it down to its core elements. I believe that virtually any business would benefit greatly from Dave's unique perspective.

Richard Singer,
Best Practice Chair, Vistage International

Dave not only understands these new tools, he also understands how to improve business performance using them. I unequivocally recommend Dave Nelsen for any business seeking to use social to grow profits.

Karl Schieneman,
Esq., ED Analytics & Review, ReviewLess LLC

Given his experience as a CEO and social media pioneer, Dave creates successful new media strategies that escape those who aren't fluent in both the corporate and new media worlds.

Paul Furiga,
President and CEO, WordWrite LLC

I highly recommend Dave as the rare, true expert in social media; he provides a unique and practical perspective into how to utilize these tools for business advantage.

Frederick D. Potthoff,
President, Kroff Chemical

Dave Nelsen has mastered the science of using social networking and social media for helping companies create conversations that build their brand, create loyalty, and achieve competitive advantage.

Razi Imam,
Founder & CEO, 113 Industries

Dave Nelsen possesses a truly profound understanding of both new communication technology and exactly how that technology can impact group dynamics and behavior in society and in business.

Ian Sadler,
President, Miller Centrigual Casting

HOW CAN I CAPITALIZE ON SOCIAL MEDIA WHEN MY KID HAS TO PROGRAM MY DVR?

THE BUSY EXECUTIVE'S GUIDE TO THE NEW TOOLS FOR BUILDING EVERY BUSINESS

Dave Nelsen

This book was written and published in partnership with inCredible Messages, LP - www.inCredibleMessages.com

HOW CAN I CAPITALIZE ON SOCIAL MEDIA WHEN MY KID HAS TO PROGRAM MY DVR?

THE BUSY EXECUTIVE'S GUIDE TO THE NEW TOOLS FOR BUILDING EVERY BUSINESS

To contact the author, Dave Nelsen, visit

Website .... www.DialogConsulting.com
　　　　　　　　　　or
　　　　　　　　　　www.DaveNelsen.com

LinkedIn .... www.linkedin.com/in/DaveNelsen

Twitter .... @davenelsen

Blog .... http://DialogConsulting.com/social-media-for-business-blog/

Google+: .... https://plus.google.com/+DaveNelsen1/posts

To contact the publisher, inCredible Messages Press, visit www.inCredibleMessages.com.

Printed in the United States of America
ISBN 978-0-9908265-0-7 paperback
ISBN 978-0-9889266-9-1 eBook

Book shepherd .... Bonnie Budzowski, inCredible Messages, LP

Cover design .... Chris Vendilli, ProFromGo Internet Marketing

Author photograph .. Karen Harmon, Harmon Photographers

DEDICATION

To my wife, Katherine.

Acknowledgments

None of us succeeds in life without the support of possibly hundreds of other people. I gratefully acknowledge my wonderful parents, Ed and Sue Nelsen (starting in 1960), my fabulous wife, Katherine (1982), and many great teachers, including Paul Knudsen (1976 high school chemistry). In addition, I gratefully acknowledge Harvey Wasserman, an executive recruiter who helped me discover my inner entrepreneur (1993); Andy Fraley, the best start-up partner anybody could ever have (1998); Dick Singer, who introduced me to Vistage International, a worldwide network of amazing CEOs and senior executives (2003); both Jeff Tobe and Dan Lynch, who encouraged me to become a professional speaker (2009) (public speaking is an incredibly rewarding profession that I'd not considered); Boaz (no last name required), a fellow speaker who always has and shares the next great idea; and Bonnie Budzowski, my book shepherd and coach throughout the creation of the book you hold in your hands.

CONTENTS

SECTION 2
SPECIFIC SOCIAL MEDIA TOOLS

SECTION 3
WINNING STRATEGIES FOR SOCIAL MEDIA

TECHNOLOGY ISN'T THE ENEMY;
IT'S THE SOLUTION

On an ordinary day in 2006, Tom Dixon, president of Blendtec, accidentally changed the face of advertising. He did so by making a show of power-blending odd ingredients, even though this was not a new idea at the time. In fact, I remember watching a *Saturday Night Live* skit 30 years earlier in which Dan Aykroyd was pitchman for the fictional Super Bass-o-Matic '76 product.

Holding a fish over a blender, Aykroyd said, "Yes, fish-eaters, the days of troublesome scaling, cutting and gutting are over, because Super Bass-o-Matic '76 is the tool that lets you use the whole bass with no fish waste." Aykroyd then blended the bass to a fine pulp. His lovely assistant took a swig on live television, exclaiming "Wow, that's terrific bass!"

Scan to see Dan Aykroyd and his Bass-o-Matic

The gross but incredibly funny skit lives on at Hulu. Use this link to find it: www.hulu.com/watch/19046 or scan the QR code.

Now flash forward to 2006, when Dixon and his marketing director, George Wright, faced a problem. The problem was that few potential customers had ever heard of Blendtec, though nearly everybody was familiar with Blendtec's chief competitor, Vitamix. Worse still, Blendtec had virtually no

2

How Can I Capitalize on Social Media
When My Kid Has to Program My DVR?

marketing budget. As Dixon told the newly hired Wright, "You are the marketing budget."

One day when Dixon was doing quality-assurance (QA) testing on selected blenders rolling off the production line, the happy accident occurred. Picture this: Selecting a random new machine and plugging it in, Dixon enthusiastically and repeatedly jams a long piece of 2″ × 2″ pine lumber into the whirring blades of a Blendtec blender. Sawdust flies everywhere as the blender performs admirably.

Things might have proceeded uneventfully following this unusual QA test, except that it sparked an idea in the mind of the marketing director.

Wright went on a $50 shopping spree, buying a can of Coke, one-half a roasted chicken, a sleeve of golf balls, and myriad odd items. Upon returning to the office, Wright had Dixon put on a white lab coat and start blending. Meanwhile, Wright started the video camera.

First up: The Coke and the chicken – together – created the now infamous "cochicken." Wright even tastes the blend and makes a garbled derogatory comment while the subtitle exclaims "Dang, this is good cochicken! This is the best I ever tasted!"

Wright posted this video clip and others on YouTube. Within weeks, literally millions tuned in with delight. Inadvertently, from an odd approach to QA testing, *social* opt-in, web-based viral advertising was born (or at least perfected).

Scan to see a Blendtec
blender in action

YouTube viewers (aka potential customers) loved the cochicken video and asked for more. Viewers wanted to know, "Could the blender handle the hot new iPhone?"

Dixon answered, "Absolutely."

In July 2007, the company posted a video showing how the iPhone met its match. The Blendtec blender became a sensation.

Blendtec launched www.WillItBlend.com to feature an ever-expanding series of demonstrations. By encouraging visitors to suggest ideas, the company tapped into the zeitgeist of everything hot.

Roughly three years later, Apple launched the first iPad. Dixon couldn't fit the iPad into the blender, so he smashed it in half on the blender base, folded the iPad into the blender jar, and pressed the "iBlend" button. In less than a minute, the iPad was powder! In the first week after its release, 5.1 million viewers learned what the iPad was made of. And Blendtec's blenders were 5.1 million viewers more famous.

Garden rakes, glow sticks (a must-see), diamonds (actually cubic zirconia), and even a snow ski all were conquered by the Blendtec blender. In the first three years of the Great Recession, as other companies were struggling to survive, Blendtec was struggling to keep up with rapidly increasing production demand. With no other major marketing initiatives, the company's revenues grew fivefold.

Blendtec had changed the playing field, and, as you can imagine, the marketing folks at Vitamix had no idea how to respond.

Dixon and Wright used new technology to *change the competitive game.* When the standard of commercial marketing was to travel to trade shows and advertise in industry publications, Blendtec used new technology: YouTube. Whether by genius or dumb luck, these pioneers followed fundamental principles for success in a social media world. We'll explore these principles in Chapter 3.

When it comes to your business, do you think about social media as a potential game changer that could catapult you to new levels of market leadership? Or do think about social media as a minefield you can't escape? Are you anxious because you have no idea how to navigate your way safely through the foreign terrain?

If you are anxious about social media as a minefield, this book is designed especially for you. If you want to navigate the minefield timidly but resolutely, this book is for you, too. And if you want to embrace social media as an opportunity to grow your business, this book is for you as well.

Know These Five Principles

Social media has the power to transform your business for good. For social media to work its magic, however, you'll need to understand and accept the five principles that follow. They are foundational to everything else in this book.

1. Ignoring new technology is an incredible risk.
2. Organizations that learn faster have a tremendous advantage.
3. Stronger relationships increase sales.
4. Improving employee communication and collaboration may be your single biggest opportunity.
5. Myths surrounding social media can sabotage your success.

Principle #1
Ignoring New Technology Is an Incredible Risk

While the concept of using new technology to change the game is broadly appealing, it's also downright scary. As a professional speaker specializing in social media, I spend much of my time with the owners and leaders of mid-sized businesses ($5 million to $250 million in revenues) all over the world. Virtually every week I'm somewhere else on the planet, meeting with such executives, typically in groups of 12-18. Over time, I've met more than 5,000 such people - the engines of the global economy.

As I travel around the world, I see a pattern in business-people and everyone else. As we get older, and especially as we become more successful, we tend to become more conservative. A friend of mine calls this trend PTP - protecting the pile. We want to stick with the proven tools that got us to a place of success.

It is impossible to ignore the growth and impact of social media, and we perceive it as a threat and a burden. Social media and its related technologies represent something we have to learn, something that takes time. For many of us, social media seems like a foreign language in which we suddenly must be fluent to survive. Since we're already overloaded, we want to know the bare minimum we can get away with.

For Dixon, Wright, and Blendtec, the technology surrounding YouTube was not an enemy; it was an *opportunity* that transformed their business. New technology was the force that catapulted their company into market leadership. They even had some fun in the process.

New technology can also help sustain a market leadership position. For example, on Twitter, people speak their mind in 140 characters (or fewer) nearly 500 million times per day. Hertz car-rental team members realize that people sometimes complain about their rental experiences by using their mobile phones to tweet. On Twitter, Hertz seeks out people complaining about Avis car rentals and the services of other competitors. Then Hertz responds with compelling offers to win over the dissatisfied customers.

Consider the value to Hertz of my friend Gini, a 14-year frequent and loyal Avis customer. Gini used Twitter to comment when Avis was sold out of cars at the Denver airport in 2009. A minute later, Hertz offered Gini a first-time renter discount code to use at the Denver airport. Gini decided to give Hertz a go, and to this day she continues to rent cars from Hertz. Brilliant? Exactly!

As you consider this example, you might shudder with a fear that commonly surrounds social media: the fear of losing control of the conversation. You might fear, as many business owners do, that bad reviews on social media will hurt your business. Do not fear: It turns out that all talk is good talk. Even bad reviews can help your business – they can help a customer see the business as authentic. We'll explore this in detail in Chapter 16.

Fear of technology is a mindset that might be hurting your business. Every mindset is a choice, an attitude. You can *choose* to master any technology you've been curious about.

If you don't know where to start, don't worry. Keep reading. I'll have a variety of recommendations for you. For example, in Chapter 7, I'll walk you through 11 straightforward steps to designing a compelling social media strategy that promises a high probability of success. You won't need to transform yourself into a 20-something or work 24 hours a day to make your strategy work.

Principle #2
Organizations That Learn Faster Have a Tremendous Advantage

I don't have to convince you we're in a world of accelerating change. Consider for a moment that the World Wide Web (as in http://www ...) did not exist when my Generation Y son Mike was born, in October 1990. The iPhone, and the roughly one million mobile applications (apps) that make the iPhone indispensable, have been around only since mid-2007. The first iPad arrived in 2010. Now most of us can't even imagine life without these remarkable tools.

It's time to accept that accelerating change is a constant you can count on. Those who adapt are the most likely to succeed. Those who don't adapt are almost certain to fail.

In 2009, the leading smartphone maker on the planet was Research In Motion (RIM). RIM's addictive Blackberry communication device dominated the competition, with better than a 50% market share. That year *Webster's New World College Dictionary*'s Word of the Year was *Crackberry,* a coinage that suggested the addictive nature of Blackberry use.

That same year, however, Apple and its two-year-old iPhone were reaching critical mass with the game-changing idea of apps. Instead of building all the technology inside its own four walls, Apple created the smartphone, a platform for others to build on. Apple included a store so that third-party developers could make money – lots of money. In so doing, Apple unlocked the collective power of all of us.

Once you understand the concept, the brilliance of Apple's approach is obvious. Google copied the Blackberry concept and then built on it with even more openness. Today Google's Android ecosystem surpasses Apple's iPhone ecosystem on a number of measures.

Meanwhile, Blackberry maker RIM didn't appreciate the change. While Apple and Google were learning what features - apps - from the outside world were interesting to their customers, Blackberry was still inventing entirely on its own. Between 2009 and 2012, RIM's market share fell from roughly 50% to around 4%, according to market analyst IDC.

Today millions of employees learn quickly using Google Alerts and Twitter Search, automatically tapping into the vast reservoir of information that is social media. Using *idea exchanges* (example to follow), more than 100,000 organizations discover how to deliver better products and services by listening to their customers. Countless people use RSS[1] dashboards to monitor the narrow slices of rapidly changing information that is most important in their jobs. And 275 million of us no longer learn alone, we learn from each other in 10s of thousands of LinkedIn groups – groups about our job functions, our industries, and our customers' businesses.

To get a flavor of an idea exchange, visit www.MyStarbucksIdea.com. You'll see that anyone can submit ideas to Starbucks - ideas for new products, improved customer service, etc. You'll see more than 275 ideas that Starbucks has implemented, innovations that originated in the minds of customers. It's not hard to see how this significantly improves Starbucks' competitive position relative to McDonald's and other interlopers in the premium coffee market.

Scan to see ideas
customers suggested
to Starbucks

To accelerate learning, you need to balance a positive attitude with a solid social media strategy. I'll show you how to develop your strategy in Chapter 7.

Principle #3
Stronger Relationships Increase Sales

And by the way, the sky is blue. Yes, the message in the preceding heading is obvious. Everybody in sales wants stronger relationships and more of them. But how do we get them? Social networking tools are a big part of the answer.

---

[1] RSS, an abbreviation usually said to derive from *really simple syndication,* is defined and explained in Chapter 19.

Have you ever thought about why athletes and other celebrities are chosen as advertising pitchmen and -women? It's a little weird, if you really think about it.

Because we spend time watching celebrities, we feel as if we know them. Because we feel as though we know them, we tend to trust them. Because we tend to trust them, we're likely to buy what they recommend.

Celebrities may be good at one thing - whatever made them famous - and in many cases are really bad at many other things. And they're actually being *paid* to sell us something. We know this, and yet we buy. It shouldn't be this way, but it is.

It turns out that this *trust effect* happens not just when we watch but also when we read. As such, something as basic as blogging - in a personal way - helps people get to know us ... and trust us.

In addition, a *media halo effect* happens to bloggers and other producers of online content. The media halo is similar to the halo we have always conferred on authors of books. Almost everyone an author meets is impressed simply because the author has written a book. It turns out that we humans also confer a halo to the bloggers we follow online.

What if that blogger were you? You could build business relationships on a scale you've never before imagined.

Another angle on relationships and social networking involves connection: Have you ever considered how many people are known by the people you know?

Most of us know roughly 150 people quite well. But LinkedIn shows us that, on average, a businessperson knows about 500 people to whom he or she can link *to* bidirectionally. If you connect with 500 people on LinkedIn, those 500 people - your *connectors* - are connected with

250,000 people, who are your so-called *second-degree connections*.

Consider the value of your connectors. If you want to get introduced to any prospect - a potential customer - among these 250,000 second-degree connections, there's the old way and the new way to make the introduction happen.

The old way is a cold call:

> Hello, my name is Dave Nelsen. I'm some social media guy you've never heard of, but I can help your company develop a compelling social media strategy to dramatically increase revenues.

That's a voice mail message that will never get a response.

Here's the new way: My connector, who actually knows me and the person with whom I desire to connect, calls on my behalf and says

> There's this social media guy, Dave Nelsen, who can help your company develop a compelling social media strategy to dramatically increase revenues.

That introduction will likely get you an in-person meeting.

Which game do you want your Sales Team to play? Social networking can help you identify and leverage hundreds of times more relationships than you currently utilize.

Principle #4
Improving Employee Communication and Collaboration May Be Your Single Biggest Opportunity

I'm guessing that, although you may have sent a telegram sometime in your life, you haven't done so in decades. You probably used to wear a pager but don't any longer. Maybe you had a Blackberry back in the day, but that's retired now. Perhaps you still send or receive the occasional fax but not as frequently as in the past.

Communication tools evolve, and we must adopt newer tools when they create new efficiencies. That's why we started using email.

However, we now spend more than 40% of our business days processing email, much of which is spam. I say it's time to look for the next new efficiencies.

In fact, two new strategies (and associated tools) can dramatically improve communication and collaboration among employees: closed *group* texting (Yammer and Chatter) and *group* information sharing (TWiki). These approaches save time compared to emailing, and they result in faster access (52% on average) to better-quality information. I'll discuss these in upcoming chapters.

Successfully embracing social media technology means regularly reviewing new technologies to learn if they present an opportunity to move forward or not - both inside and outside your company.

Fortunately, embracing social media doesn't necessarily mean you must master every new service as it comes down the pike. It doesn't mean you must keep piling one new technology on top of another until you smother yourself and everyone who works for you under the heap. In fact, it's impossible to add new tools and activities continually, without reducing or eliminating the use of older ones.

Learning to use the tools that offer opportunity *externally* can move your business forward in big ways. Adopt them before and apply them better than your competitors.

At the same time, it's essential to evaluate new tools as opportunities to bring net productivity gains *internally*. Many of the new tools are more effective for communicating than the ones we've come to rely on. Find those tools and make it a priority to adopt them.

As you adopt new social media tools that make sense for your business, choose the tools and activities it makes sense to terminate. Remember that eliminating old habits is as hard as adopting new habits.

Chapters throughout this book will help you to evaluate technologies in light of your specific situation. Chances are you'll be surprised at the things you can let go.

Principle #5
Myths Surrounding Social Media Can Sabotage Your Success

As I talk to leaders of medium-sized businesses all over the world, I encounter the following myths repeatedly:

- ❐ Social media is a tool only for Generations X and Y (those born from 1964 to 2000, who are known as digital natives).
- ❐ Social media is not important for companies that sell business to business (B2B).
- ❐ Social media takes an impossible amount of time.

Not one of these myths is true! With the increasing impact of social media on business success, it's ridiculous to ignore this technology merely because you happen to be born before 1964. Such a tactic might well be the death of your life's work.

It's time to find your courage, step up, and discover a powerful tool for your own success. Once you honestly look for the power in social media, you'll discover that it has promise for any business, including B2B. If you follow my advice throughout these pages, you'll also discover that social media does not have to consume an impossible amount of time. Used strategically, social media tools will save you time as well as bring you customers.

One of my primary goals in writing this book is to convince you that social media technology isn't the enemy;

it's the solution. Like email relative to the telegram, social media tools can be more efficient and more effective for some of our communication and marketing challenges. If we learn how, when, and where to use these tools, they can actually save us time. And if we learn these things before our competitors do, we most certainly will win while they lose.

HOW TO USE THIS BOOK

This isn't the type of book in which you have to read every word. You can flip directly to the chapters that cover tools that interest you. At the same time, there's more in this book than guidance on specific social media tools.

I've divided the book into three sections.

Section 1: Chapters 2 to 7
The Big Picture and Foundational Principles of Success in Social Media

These chapters provide the knowledge you need to use social media tools successfully. These are foundational chapters, and I encourage you to read them before you begin flipping through the chapters about specific tools.

In each of the first five chapters, I'll develop the big ideas that can help you use social media to accelerate learning and enhance communication. In Chapter 6, I'll uncover 10 social media mistakes you'll want to avoid at all costs. In Chapter 7, I'll guide you through the process of making a social media plan that is customized for your business.

You might think of this first section of chapters as a Google map of the "world of mouth." These chapters will give you the 50,000-foot view of the entire planet so that you understand the big picture.

Section 2: Chapters 8 to 17
Specific Social Media Tools

Each chapter in this section will explore a specific tool, taking you on a visit to "countries" on the map, including LinkedIn, Facebook, Yammer, WordPress, GetSatisfaction, Chatter, TWiki, Google+, Ning, and so on. Each of these chapters stands on its own. You can read the chapters sequentially or randomly, based on your most pressing issues and opportunities.

Section 3: Chapters 18 to 23
Winning Strategies for Social Media

These chapters will guide you to consider how to use social media in effective and strategic ways. Chapter 18 will help you use customer testimonials effectively. Chapter 19 will explore how to use an RSS dashboard to reduce information overload. Chapter 20 will help you to stop fearing your critics and use them to advantage. Chapter 21 will show you, step-by-step, how to decide if the next new hot service is for you (or if you can happily ignore it). Chapter 22 will provide a blueprint for true social media success: converting visitors, Likers, and followers into customers. Chapter 23 will wrap things up and issue your call to action.

If you're not convinced that you need the power of social media, just read the story at the beginning of the next chapter. It's a real eye-opener.

What Not to Blend

One day things didn't work out so well at Blendtec. Picture this:

George Wright purchases a Contractor Pack of 100 box-cutter razor blades. In their original packaging, the razor blades jam the blender, so Tom Dixon places a piece of paper over the top of the blender jar, spreads the blades on top of the paper, places the jar cover on top of that, and uses his hand to hold it down. After firing up the blender, he pulls the paper away like a magician pulling a table-cloth from under a perfectly set table.

Blendtec's blender jar is made of bulletproof polycarbonate. However, the blender jar cover is a different story; it's made of thin, flexible black plastic.

The problem is immediately obvious. Tom pulls his hand away as fragments of razor blades start shooting through the plastic. A second later, the top flies off the blender and Dixon and his camera operator run from the room.

The blender is set to turn off automatically after 40 seconds. Dixon returns to walls and ceiling covered with sharp metal fragments. While a disaster restoration team is ultimately able to salvage these surfaces, the carpeting is a different matter. It's a total loss and must be replaced.

CHAPTER 1 SUMMARY

☐ When it comes to responding to the exponential rate of change we all face: Technology isn't the enemy; it's the solution.

☐ Successful companies are using new social tools to change the game. You can too. For an example, check out how Blendtec first used YouTube in 2006 to achieve competitive advantage over competitors.

☐ Social media has the power to transform your business positively. For social media to work its magic, you need to accept the following principles:

- Ignoring new technology is an incredible risk. Adapting to and embracing change increases your probability of business success.

- In a world of accelerating change, organizations that learn faster than others will have a tremendous advantage. Social media tools can dramatically accelerate learning.

- To increase sales, you need stronger relationships and more of them. Social networking can help you identify and leverage hundreds of times more relationships than you currently utilize.

- Effective internal communication, among employees, is usually even more important than effective external communication. Social networking tools can radically improve employee communication and collaboration.

- The myths surrounding social media can sabotage your success. Contrary to popular belief, social media tools can actually save you time and money.

THE BIG PICTURE AND FOUNDATIONAL PRINCIPLES OF SUCCESS IN SOCIAL MEDIA

CHAPTER 2

SILENCE (NOT TECHNOLOGY) IS THE ENEMY; WHY YOU NEED TO EMBRACE THE CONVERSATION

In 2008, musician Dave Carroll was traveling from Halifax, Nova Scotia, to a destination in Nebraska. He was flying on United Airlines. When connecting through Chicago's O'Hare Airport, Carroll watched the baggage crew abusing his precious Taylor guitar as the crew loaded his plane. He complained to three flight attendants, who showed "complete indifference" about the rough treatment. Upon claiming his baggage in Nebraska, Carroll discovered to his horror that his guitar had incurred serious damage.

Carroll dutifully got an estimate for the repair cost and filed a corresponding $1,200 claim with the airline. United denied the claim. Carroll appealed. Upon each subsequent denial of the claim, Carroll persisted and escalated, ultimately working up to the United Airlines VP of Customer Service, almost one year later. When the VP said no, Carroll embarked on Plan B.

Scan to see *United Breaks Guitars*

Employees of United Airlines apparently thought they could ignore Carroll's complaint without consequence. Wrong! Carroll's Plan B was to put the event to song (remember, he's a musician). He posted the song on YouTube on July 6, 2009 (http://bit.ly/united-airlines-breaks-guitars). Because the creative and entertaining video complaint resonated

with air travelers (whose luggage hasn't been abused by baggage handlers?), it went viral as people shared it with their
friends.

Ten million views later, one analyst estimated that Carroll's video had cost United Airlines $180,000,000 in brand
damage. Today, 63,441 people have used the YouTube icon to
Like the video vs. 1,254 who chose the Dislike icon. A recent
snarky comment suggests that 1,253 of those Dislikes must be
by United Airlines employees. Indeed.

The sequels to Carroll's video, *United Breaks Guitars
Song 2,* and especially *United Breaks Guitars Song 3*, are
among my favorite videos on the Web.

The reach of social media gives unhappy customers, former employees, and wronged partners power they didn't have
before. Don't kid yourself into believing you can be silent in
the face of stakeholder dissatisfaction. Like it or not, this hot
sauce is out of the bottle; there's no way to put it back. You
can't afford to ignore the shift in power that has come with social media.

Engaging in conversations may be uncomfortable because
you are no longer solely in control, but you can't afford to be
silent. Your silence just allows someone else to control the
conversation about you.

DON'T WORRY: ALMOST ALL TALK IS GOOD TALK

In the summer of 2010, Hollywood Video, the last DVD rental
store in my neighborhood, went kaput. My sons started advo-
cating for Netflix, and I knew exactly where that was going. I
didn't want to be mailing DVDs back and forth, so I resisted.

"Dad, don't worry. You don't need to mail DVDs anymore. Netflix can stream videos straight to our Xbox 360 and
Wii." So we signed up.

Seeing this fabulous streaming video service in my sons'
game room, I wanted it in my home theater. The problems
were that my projection TV didn't support Netflix and my

Internet router was 2½ floors away. So I googled "Netflix Wi-Fi HDMI," meaning "How do I get Netflix over Wi-Fi (wirelessly) to the HDMI input port on my projection TV?"

The top result was for a company called Roku, which sold a little box that could do exactly what I needed. After reading an overview, I clicked to the product page to explore the features in more detail. To my surprise, I found that Roku had neatly organized more than 1,000 negative reviews of their product on the very page where they were trying to get me to click on "Buy."

A strange thing happened. Instead of going next to CNET reviews or to *Consumer Reports* or querying my Facebook friends to see what they thought, I read a few dozen comments, including those that were ranked "Most Negative." Then I clicked on Buy.

Negative information actually accelerated my purchase decision because I believed I had an authentic understanding of the product. I could accept the so-called shortcomings (e.g., "This d*** product took 15 minutes to configure, not the claimed 5").

Consider this question: Is it better for your customers to understand the reality of your products and services before or after they buy? Since they'll ultimately discover the realties, I say it's better that it happen sooner rather than later. In fact, I'd rather not acquire customers who won't be satisfied in the end.

Companies that are embracing authentic reviews are experiencing lower product return rates, in some cases 45% lower or even lower. Think about it. Not only is this a huge cost savings, it eliminates a whole class of unhappy customers who would otherwise be impugning the companies' reputations with their billion+ Facebook friends.

In business, we assume that, when people say bad things about us, we have a problem. Indeed, the opposite is true - if we take advantage of it.

Next time talk turns negative, recognize that it's a trifecta opportunity for your company:

1. *Aggressively address the situation.* Try to turn the situation around. Remember, a customer who had a problem that is satisfactorily resolved will have a higher lifetime value to your company than a customer who never had a problem (or at least who never talked about it.)

2. *Demonstrate responsiveness.* Even if you can't turn a problem around for a specific customer, you can show everybody else how responsive your team is. In essence, help those people understand what your products really can and can't do.

3. *Use the experience to learn.* Consider each experience an opportunity to avoid similar problems in the future. Maybe you can avoid problems by making product improvements, enhancing your customer support, or enabling authentic reviews. Learning that leads to change leads to more happy customers in the end.

We Need Everyone's Smarts to Win

I wonder if you've heard this old Japanese expression: *None of us is as smart as all of us.* This has become a mantra for me, and I'll repeat it often throughout this book. I first experienced the *none of us* effect in 1987, when I was promoted into first-line management at AT&T Bell Labs.

At the time, all new managers attended a one-week training program to learn how to manage people (in a single week!). One exercise from the experience still stands out for me. The exercise is known as The Desert Survival Exercise, which was developed by Human Synergistics International.

The 30 of us in the class were asked to imagine that we'd just survived an airplane crash in the desert. We were given a list of 15 items to prioritize, without consulting each other, based on each item's importance to our collective survival.

The items included one pair of sunglasses (per person), a magnetic compass, two quarts of 180-proof vodka (an obvious top priority), a cosmetic mirror, a jackknife, a plastic raincoat, a book about edible animals of the desert, and so on.

After each of us had ranked the items from top to bottom, we were arranged into six groups of five people each and asked to develop a consensus ranking within 15 minutes. Lots of rancor ensued as team members argued the merits of their respective choices. Through discussion and compromise, each group produced a consensus list.

You may be surprised to learn that there is an "ideal" ranking of the items, according to desert survival expert Alonzo W. Pond. The participants scored our individual and team lists against the expert's ordering. Something amazing happened.

Every single group produced a better team ranking than any individual within the group had produced alone. The odds of that happening seemed astronomical to me. I was tempted to believe this was a fluke until another day, when I played a similar ranking exercise. The exercise, Lost in the Arctic, produced the same surprising outcome.

Indeed, *none of us is as smart as all of us.* This is a primary reason that the strategic use of social media can give us a competitive advantage. To succeed, we need to be involved in conversation. We need to engage others in sharing knowledge so that together we can be smarter than any individual. Social media connects us through dialogue to make us collectively smarter.

TALKING IS THE SECRET TO INCREASING KNOWLEDGE

Remember the old parable about the blind men and the elephant? To be politically correct, let's call it the parable of the visually impaired humans and the pachyderm.

It goes like this: Six visually impaired humans are touching a pachyderm in different places and arguing about what they have. Each person is convinced he or she knows the answer, based on sensory experience. The person holding the trunk has a snake. The one below the ear senses a fan. The one holding the tusk has a spear. The one with the leg has a tree trunk. The person holding the tail has a rope. The one pushing on the creature's body feels an immovable wall. Each participant is sure of having the right answer.

The issue here is not that the people are visually impaired. It's that each person has valid but incomplete information, only a small portion of the picture. This is the human condition: limited perspective. The problem arises when the humans in the parable draw firm conclusions based on incomplete data. The problem arises when they fail to communicate and integrate what each knows respectively. Is it possible social media can help us solve such problems?

For an example, look to Twitter. As you may know, Twitter is the service that allows you to send a text message (a tweet) of up to 140 characters to the cloud (the Internet), using a mobile device or virtually any computer. Once posted to the cloud, anyone can choose to read your tweet and/or follow your future tweets. Almost 500 million such messages are posted each day.

Let's observe as a conversation on Twitter unfolds. (Twitter is easy to use, as you'll see in the example) Watch how a group of people, each communicating limited information, comes up with an amazing discovery.

The Twitter conversation begins May 1, 2011, at 1 a.m. in Pakistan.

Sohaib (pronounced "sue-HA-bee") Athar, a regular guy few people had heard of, using the Twitter name ReallyVirtual, tweets

> ReallyVirtual: *Helicopter hovering above Abbottabad at 1 AM (is a rare event).*

When the time is 1 a.m. in Pakistan, it is 4 p.m. in Washington, D.C. This tweet is posted at the same time that President

Obama and his team crowd into a small conference room next to the White House Situation Room to watch real-time video of SEAL Team Six taking out Osama Bin Laden. The time is an interesting point: President Obama will not brief the American public and the world until 6½ hours later. See what happens on Twitter in the meantime.

> ReallyVirtual: *Go away helicopter – before I take out my giant swatter :-/*

> ReallyVirtual: *A huge window shaking bang here in Abbottabad, Cantt. I hope it's not the start of something nasty :-S*

At this point, another Twitter user, Mohcin Shah (Twitter name m0hcin), likely monitoring references to Abbottabad because his family lives there, becomes alarmed about his loved ones' safety. Even though it's the middle of the night in Abbottabad, he calls family members and then reports

> m0hcin: *Just talked to family in Abbottabad, say they heard three blasts one after another, don't know what really happened.*

We now have two visually impaired humans touching the elephant. In this case, although they've never met, they begin communicating, pooling their collective knowledge. Specifically, m0hcin directs a question to ReallyVirtual by placing the @ sign before his user name, the standard convention for communicating publicly with a specific person on Twitter.

> m0hcin: *@ReallyVirtual Hello Sir, any update on the blasts? What has really happened?*

ReallyVirtual answers m0hcin directly, in the same fashion (using @):

> ReallyVirtual: *@m0hcin All silent after the blast, but a friend heard it 6 km away... the helicopter is gone too.*

Perhaps alerted by another friend who was watching this dialogue, ReallyVirtual shares a link to an article just posted on
the Web by Pakistan News about an apparent helicopter crash
near the military academy at Kakul.

> ReallyVirtual: *@m0hcin http://bit.ly/ljB6p6 Seems
> like my giants swatter worked!*

> ReallyVirtual: *@m0hcin the few people online at this
> time of night are saying one of the copters was not
> Pakistani...*

An apparent friend, Hassan Rai (raihak), now joins the conversation:

> raihak: *@ReallyVirtual be safe!*

> ReallyVirtual: *@raihak I try, man, I try*

> ReallyVirtual: *@raihak Funny, moving to Abbotta-
> bad was part of the 'being safe' strategy*

ReallyVirtual now deliberately opens the conversation to more
people by creating a hashtag referencing Abbottabad (#abbot-
tabad). In Twitter, a hashtag is a signaling mechanism, telling
people how to connect their messages to a specific conversation. In this case, those watching the current conversation can
connect their messages to it by including the hashtag #abbot-
tabad.

> ReallyVirtual: *Since taliban (probably) don't have
> helicopters, and since they're saying it was not
> 'ours', must be a complicated situation #abbottabad*

Using Twitter Search (https://twitter.com/search-home) ReallyVirtual (and everyone else) can now monitor tweets worldwide that include the hashtag #abbottabad. In essence, ReallyVirtual accelerates his rate of learning by creating a global
dialogue. Roughly 60 minutes into events, he summarizes
what he knows.

> ReallyVirtual: *The Abbottabad helicopter/UFO was
> shot down near the Bilil Town area, and there's re-
> port of a flash. People saying it could be a drone.*

Another person, Tahir Akram (tahirakram), shows up and immediately repeats the message almost verbatim, attributing it to ReallyVirtual. Tahirakram does this because he knows he has a different group of followers who may be interested. Notice that many tweets – in fact, the vast majority on Twitter – are not directed to anyone.

> tahirakram: *Abbottabad helicopter/UFO was shot down near Bilil Town and there's report of a flash. People saying it could be a drone. via @ReallyVirtual*

> ReallyVirtual: *@tahirakram yea. *hides his giant swatter**

> tahirakram: *Anything good the intelligence agencies are doing?*

> ReallyVirtual: *@tahirakram Very likely – but it was too noisy to be a spy craft, or a very poor spy craft it was.*

> ReallyVirtual: *Here's the location of the Abbottabad crash according to some people >>>* http://on.fb.me/khjf34

The link is to a screenshot of a Google map on ReallyVirtual's iPhone. He had posted the map on Facebook. Notice that the time is now 2:22 a.m. local time, less than 90 minutes into the operation. Can you imagine the CIA trying to conduct a covert operation in a world of Twitter?

> ReallyVirtual: *Two helicopters, one down, could actually be the training accident scenario they're saying it was* >> http://bit.ly/ioGE60

> ReallyVirtual: *and now I feel I must apologize to the pilot about the swatter tweets :-/*

The conversation continues like this for several hours, with the audience building from a handful of people to literally 10s of thousands. At around 9:30 p.m. Eastern Time, an hour before President Obama will appear on television, CNN announces that there will be a breaking news address by the president.

At this point, someone new but relatively obscure, Munzir Naqvi (naqvi), makes a connection.

> naqvi: *I think the helicopter crash in Abbottabad, Pakistan and the President Obama breaking news address are connected.*

ReallyVirtual sees the message because it contains the word Abbottabad, and then he repeats (on Twitter to repeat is to retweet, or RT) it so that the message is seen not just by naqvi's few followers, but also by the nearly 100,000 people now following ReallyVirtual's conversation.

> ReallyVirtual: *RT @naqvi: I think the helicopter crash in Abbottabad, Pakistan and the President Obama breaking news address are connected.*

Yet another Twitter user, Saad, using the Twitter handle kursed, adds more information:

> kursed: *Geo is also reporting evidence of two US spec op choppers which conducted this operation in Abbottabad.*

> ReallyVirtual: *@kursed Another rumor: two copters that followed the crashed one were foreign Cobras – and got away.*

Notice that early in the dialogue, the helicopters were identified only as "foreign" but that now they're being described as

American and references to them include tweeters' guesses about the helicopter model.

> ReallyVirtual: @kursed I think I should take out my big blower to blow the fog of war away and see the clearer picture.

With so many people around the world now following ReallyVirtual, it is inevitable that this wish is realized. One Twitter user, iSuckBigTime, provides a compelling piece of information, which is immediately retweeted by ReallyVirtual:

> ReallyVirtual: RT @iSuckBigTime: Osama Bin Laden killed in Abbottabad Pakistan: ISI has confirmed it.

ISI is Pakistan's Inter-Services Intelligence, a solidly credible source. To the message, ReallyVirtual adds

> ReallyVirtual: << Uh oh, there goes the neighborhood.

Bradley Burgess (BradleyK8Olsen) chimes in, followed by Chris Hoy Poy (kryanth):

> BradleyK8Olsen: Abbottabad just became a sexy new spring break destination.

> Kryanth: How long before the 'Call of Duty: Abbottabad, Pakistan' expansion hits the stores?

Kryanth has just named a video game of the future[2] while most Americans have not ever heard the word *Abbottabad*. Only after this entire dialogue on Twitter (and far more that I've not included) does President Obama appear on TV to talk about what those talking on Twitter already know.

---

[2] The game will ultimately be called Medal of Honor: Warfighter. Seven members of the SEAL Team Six will be disciplined for providing classified information to the game producer, Electronic Arts Inc.

This Twitter conversation is the perfect illustration of what can happen when the visually impaired humans experiencing the pachyderm actually communicate. It demonstrates that *all of us are much smarter than any of us.* No one in the conversation had more than slivers of information. Yet the participants put their information together into an amazingly accurate whole. The whole went far beyond what any individual in the conversation could possibly have known.

Notice how the sharing of information on Twitter differs from conversations via email. In fact, there are four major differences:

1. *The Twitter messages are concise.* While messages can include links to documents and images, Twitter messages are limited to 140 characters.

2. *Twitter participants use powerful new tools.* For example, hashtags and global search allow users to find and organize information in new ways.

3. *Unlike email, Twitter messages are usually not sent to specific individuals.* The content producers post their messages to the cloud, and the content consumers decide who to follow. This is a 180° paradigm flip from email. Content producers of email choose the content consumers by specifying email addresses.

4. *Twitter conversations are conducted publicly, unlocking individual minds to create collective knowledge.* If this conversation had been conducted via email, we couldn't be exploring it now.

The real importance of the Abbottabad example is not in the specific event, but in appreciating the power of social networking tools in action. Apply to your business the metaphor of the visually impaired humans touching pachyderms.

Each of your employees has a unique perspective on your customers, your products, your competitors, and on the marketplace. So why not have your employees jump on Twitter and start sharing what each knows about customers, prospects, competitors, and products? What could happen if the entire team shares information?

Of course, it would be crazy to share proprietary information on a public forum like Twitter. But what if there were a private version of this service for corporate use?

There is. It's called Yammer (www.Yammer.com), and it's now in use by more than 100,000 organizations. Yammer functions just like Twitter but offers private messaging within an organization.[3] Yammer features the same powerful functions as Twitter (hashtags, global search, ubiquitous access, etc.) and the same advantages

Scan to try Yammer

relative to email communication. Salesforce offers a similar tool, called Chatter (www.salesforce.com/chatter/overview/), which is equally popular.

Bill Gates predicts that social networking–type apps are likely to replace email as the dominant form of corporate communication. Putting his money where his mouth is, Microsoft purchased Yammer in the summer of 2012. So we're likely to see Yammer-style functionality become a part of the Microsoft Office suite.

If your only forms of internal communication are meetings, phone calls, and email, chances are you're missing huge opportunities for learning and synergy. Imagine how a service like Yammer or Chatter could connect your field people with the experts in your organization. Imagine how it could mobilize your team to detect and resolve customer issues more quickly. On the other hand, imagine your competitors

---

[3] Yammer allows an administrator to invite outside parties into a network. Yammer also has a variety of other features allowing subgroup communication and even one-to-one messaging.

adopting these tools before you do. What can you gain and what can you lose by ignoring social media?

Consider putting Yammer or Chatter to work in your organization. Companies that have are reporting

- ❐ 39% improvement in collaboration.
- ❐ 52% faster access to information.
- ❐ 30% drop in email - roughly one hour per day per employee. Some of that time is going into Yammer or Chatter, but not all of it.
- ❐ 27% fewer meetings.

Yes, social media tools can actually save you more time than they take. And improve results.

Communications tools evolve continuously. We're no longer sending telegrams to each other. Could it be that email is the telegram of our day? Ask a 20-year-old for his or her opinion.

In the next chapter, I'll provide three simple rules for joining the social media conversation.

Use Screenshots to Enhance Your Messages

Like Sohaib Athar, sometimes I want to share a map. Or I want to save an article I'm reading in *The Wall Street Journal.* In such situations, it's incredibly handy to take a picture of the screen of my mobile device.

On an iPad or iPhone, you can do this by simultaneously pressing the Home (circular) and Power buttons for a fraction of a second. You'll find the resulting image in your camera roll.

On the newer Android phones (releases 4.0 and later), press the volume-down and Power buttons simultaneously.

In the lower-left area of most Android tablets (including the Samsung Galaxy Tab 10.1), there's an icon that looks like an expanding rectangle. Touch it to capture the screen.

They're Writing About You

There's a site where, typically, *former* employees go to write about their employers. It's called Glassdoor (www.Glassdoor.com).

Are you curious about what a Starbucks store manager makes? Don't be; it's on Glassdoor: $43,000 per year. Wondering what employees think of Goldman Sachs? Average rating 3.8 out of 5 (not bad for an investment bank, given public sentiment following the Great Recession).

This past summer I talked with a recent college graduate who was entering one of the toughest employment environments in a generation. He told me that he had an invitation to interview at a company. The graduate looked up the company on Glassdoor and didn't want to work at "a place like that." Without even talking to him, the company lost a great prospective employee.

Your former employees are affecting your ability to hire future talent. So why leave the matter exclusively in their hands? Encourage your current employees to write reviews. Get the whole story out there. And think about how you can make your company an even better place to work, because now it's a glass door. There are no secrets in a social media world.

CHAPTER 2 SUMMARY

☐ Silence is the enemy. Now is the time to embrace the social media conversation.

☐ Ignoring unhappy customers, as United Airlines ignored musician Dave Carroll, can have dire consequences.

☐ All talk is good talk because it creates authenticity that brings us the right customers and excludes the wrong ones. And talk accelerates the rate of learning.

☐ When someone complains, it's a trifecta opportunity. You have the opportunity to address the situation with the specific client, to everyone else you can demonstrate your responsiveness, and you have the opportunity to learn from the incident.

☐ We need everyone's smarts to win. *None of us is as smart as all of us.*

☐ Twitter, Yammer, and Chatter differ from email in four critical ways.

1. They are concise.
2. They incorporate powerful new tools.
3. They are sent to the crowd rather than specific individuals.
4. They unlock collective intelligence rather than individual minds.

☐ Social networking–type apps are likely to replace email as the dominant form of corporate communication. Now is the time to adopt some of these new tools, before your competitors do.

CHAPTER 3

Social Media Conversations Improve Your Products While Filling Your Pipeline

Your customers' experiences with your products and services are far broader than those of your employees. Why not harvest customers' ideas in an organized manner? The term for this is *crowdsourcing,* and you can do it. You can harvest customer experiences via Facebook, Twitter, blogs, LinkedIn groups, idea exchanges, and more.

Conversations Lead to Business-Boosting Ideas

I first experienced my favorite application of crowdsourcing in early 2010. Visiting my local Starbucks, I noticed a small sign on the corkboard: "Got an idea for us? Tell us at www.MyStarbucksIdea.com." Upon returning to my office, I went to the site to make my first suggestion. In order to participate, I was required to share a few basic details about myself, including my name and my email address. Easy enough.

As I mentioned briefly in Chapter 1, I was interested in Starbucks' *idea exchange,* an evolution of the good ole suggestion box, with healthy doses of brainstorming, focus groups, and democracy mixed in. As the weeks marched by, I watched hundreds of different ideas flooding in from other Starbucks customers. Some were intriguing. Others were blatantly self-serving. For example, "Please arrange for a bus stop and shelter for me in front of my local Starbucks."

But I didn't just watch. Starbucks' idea exchange is a democracy, so I voted on the ideas of others, promoting those I liked and demoting those I didn't. Rather than assuming a spectator role, I became hooked on participating.

With growing interest and curiosity, I kept returning to the site to see which ideas were gaining momentum. Then something amazing happened. I received an email from Starbucks: "Dave, here are the first 50 ideas we've implemented based on your suggestions."

I thought, "Wow. I'm a valued participant! Starbucks is listening to me." And I kept giving my ideas and voting on the ideas of others.

In October 2010, I received an update on the first 100 ideas implemented from the minds of Starbucks customers. In August 2011, Starbucks reached 150 ideas. In June 2012, the company crossed the 200-idea mark. In April 2013, it cracked 275 ideas.

Did I mention that only 271 of the ideas Starbucks considered came from me? Other people on the planet also helped guide Starbucks. Two of my favorite ideas are the plastic green stick and the reusable sleeve. Here is how these came to be.

Have you ever ordered a venti Americano with room, half-caf, no whip, but with some soy, and some Splenda? (Yes, a Starbucks drive-through has a language all its own.) Then you placed your precious coffee in your automobile cup holder as you drove away? And then, when you hit a bump just right, a geyser of coffee erupted from that small hole in the lid?

The baristas who work for Starbucks don't have this geyser problem because the stores don't move (those in California sometimes being an exception). Only drive-through customers experience this problem. Only customers had the information Starbucks needed to improve their customer experience in this area.

On the idea exchange, one person suggested that Starbucks make something to snap into the hole to stop the splashing.

Someone else suggested that, if the something were long, it could double as a stirrer. This was a popular idea, and everyone started promoting it. The next thing I knew, Starbucks launched that now ubiquitous green stick. Their customers gave them the idea free, on the idea exchange.

While they were talking about takeout coffee, Starbucks customers asked why the company had to double-cup or use insulating cardboard sleeves on their Americanos. Customers made and promoted another suggestion: Instead of filling up landfills with this stuff, make a reusable sleeve, sell it for $3, and we'll all save the planet together. Starbucks made the sleeve, lowering its own costs in the process. That's genius: the customers' genius (and Starbucks' genius for listening).

Any business can be more effective in serving its customers when the people behind the business understand customers' pain points and priorities. An idea exchange is an effective way to uncover your customers' implicit needs and desires, through explicit suggestions. Further, the exchange, through the voting process, drives the ideas with widest appeal to the surface, so your Product Team or Service Development Team can allocate limited resources to the most important market opportunities.

Good news: You don't have to be a big fish like Starbucks to host an idea exchange.

SOCIAL MEDIA CONVERSATIONS WORK IN B2C AND B2B

The Starbucks idea exchange represents a B2C (business-to-consumer) example. Such a tool is equally effective in B2B (business-to-business) applications – as long as you have a critical mass of interested participants. As a rule of thumb, an audience of 1,000 or more constitutes a critical mass.

For example, for more than 10 years I've been a member of Vistage International, a network of more than 15,000 business executives. Like me, the majority of Vistage member companies sell B2B. That makes Vistage itself essentially a B2B2B organization.

Vistage exists to help business executives become better leaders, which means they make better decisions and get better results. For a full day every month, members meet, in groups of 12–18, to work *on* their businesses instead of *in* their businesses. As such, it should come as no surprise that Vistage member companies substantially outperform their peers in any economy.

Vistage International continuously works to serve its members better. So, like Starbucks, it runs an idea exchange. However, unlike Starbucks, it runs the exchange in a closed, private network called Vistage Village so that competitors cannot see (and steal) the innovative ideas being discussed.

One of the biggest innovations resulting from Vistage's idea exchange was a dramatic redesign of the Vistage Village member portal. In its first incarnation, the portal was so packed with information that it was overwhelming. Through suggestions and voting, members "surfaced" the features and content that were most important to them. When Vistage Village 2.0 was launched, it provided direct access to the reduced subset of information of greatest importance to members, once again proving the old saw that less is more.

To those doing a casual search, B2B applications are hard - or even impossible - to find, because these applications are not aimed at mass audiences. However, it is a mistake to conclude that, because we see only the B2C examples, such tools are of no value in the B2B context. In reality, the B2B examples are almost endless.

For example, Salesforce (https://success.salesforce.com) offers one of the world's premiere customer relationship management–sales force management solutions. Salesforce sells to businesses that sell to businesses (B2B2B again), typically to those with long sales cycles and strategic selling processes. To harvest ideas from customers, Salesforce runs an idea exchange that is open to all visitors; check out https://success.salesforce.com/ideaSearch.

If you like the idea exchange concept, you don't have to build yours from the ground up. In fact, you can add the technology to your website tomorrow for less than $200 per month. Different flavors of the application are available as a service from multiple providers, including

- ❒ Bright Idea (www.BrightIdea.com)
- ❒ Jive (www.JiveSoftware.com)
- ❒ Salesforce (www.salesforce.com)
- ❒ UserVoice (www.UserVoice.com)

You can also exchange ideas by means of Facebook, Twitter, blogs, LinkedIn groups, and other social media venues.

CONVERSATIONS LEAD TO BIDIRECTIONAL LEARNING AND TRUST

Social media provides many tools for creating dialogue and building trust. In a dialogue, your team learns about what existing and potential customers want and value, and those groups learn about what your company offers. Your customers learn to see your employees as people just like themselves. Such dialogue builds relationships that increase trust. Trust is the foundation for selling anything.

For example, take a brief look at a blog called *Randy's Journal,* at www.BoeingBlogs.com/randy/. A blog is simply an

Scan to see the blog
Randy's Journal

online diary or journal that invites readers to post comments or questions in response to the writer's entries.

You will find an in-depth analysis of Randy's blog and the underlying strategy in Chapter 14. For now, just take a quick look at an effective example of crowdsourcing.

As you arrive at *Randy's Journal,* you'll notice that Randy is a real person, the vice president, marketing, of Boeing Commercial Airplanes. You'll see a photo of Randy and get a sense of his personality by reading just a few posts. Through videos, you'll "meet" a variety of other people at Boeing. These people include everyone from the workers who do aircraft testing to the general manager of Boeing's Dreamliner program. You'll experience each of these individuals as people who have thoughts, feelings, and values much like your own. Boeing will take on a personality.

In *Randy's Journal,* readers learn about Boeing strategy and the issues facing the airline industry. At the same time, through reader comments and questions, Randy and his team learn more about customers and potential customers. This bidirectional learning benefits both Boeing and its audience.

Randy's Journal is not traditional push marketing. In the blog, the people who are Boeing connect with the people who are or could be Boeing's customers. In sales, there's an adage: People buy from people. A blog creates a bidirectional conversation that helps blog writers and readers understand each other. In connecting, we get to know and trust each other.

Whether you choose an idea exchange, a blog, or another social media tool, engaging in a dialogue with your customers is incredibly valuable. It's a surefire route to engaging customers, building trust, learning how to improve products and services, and participating in bidirectional learning.

SUCCESSFUL SOCIAL MEDIA CONVERSATIONS FOLLOW RULES

Social media conversations work, as long as they follow three basic rules.

Rule 1:
The Cocktail Party Rule

The norms in effect at a cocktail party apply to social media also. (I'm talking about norms *before* the third martini.) More important, the behaviors that get you into trouble at a cocktail party will get you into trouble in social media. (I learned this rule from Drew McLellan, a blogger for *Social Media Today,* one of my favorite resources.)

Scan to see Dave explaining the three rules for using social media in business.

So what do you do at a cocktail party? You meet people, engage in conversations, ask and answer questions, and build relationships. It's the same thing in social media. In short, you engage in a dialogue.

Have you ever bumped into an insurance salesperson at a cocktail party - the kind who introduces himself and then begins a long monologue all about his products? This is inappropriate behavior both at a cocktail party and in an online connection.

Social media is a time for connection, not a new channel for push marketing or overt selling. As a classic book, *Guerrilla Marketing,* reminds us, "Marketing is not about us; it's about them." This truth is even more important in social media.

At a cocktail party, it's also inappropriate to introduce yourself and then completely stop talking. The social media equivalent to this is posting a blog entry or a Facebook update and then not engaging as people join the conversation. If a reader asks you a question, you had better respond. Once you open the door, be prepared to participate. Show an interest in helping participants get what they want, and business will follow.

Rule 2: PIE

PIE is an acronym from the radio business. Before dee-jays go live, they remind each other to remember PIE. The acronym, which has worked for decades in radio, works just as well in social media.

Personality

Interesting

Entertaining

P stands for *personality.* Since social media is about people connecting with people, this element of the acronym reminds every one of us to be a real person and display some personality! To repeat the sales adage: People buy from people. That's what this whole social media effort is about – personalizing your business.

I and *E* stand for *interesting* and *entertaining,* two characteristics needed to attract and retain readers' attention. Think about it: Everybody is as busy and as distracted as you are. If you are boring, they won't pay attention to you for very long. Learn from the examples of Tom Dixon at Blendtec and Randy at Boeing.

An Unexpected Example of Entertainment

Groupon caught my attention with a surprising example of entertainment. Subscribers to Groupon receive a group coupon, or Groupon, by email every day. For example, you might be offered, for $50, a certificate worth $100 on a massage at a specific salon close to your home.

Federal law mandates that, if you do email marketing, you must have an "unsubscribe" process. Federal law does not specify that your unsubscribe process must be boring. The Groupon process to unsubscribe is a great example of PIE.

After receiving one-too-many daily Groupon offers for items I didn't need (something like 50% off hot air ballooning), I clicked on Unsubscribe.

A confirmation screen appeared: "You are unsubscribed. We're sorry to see you go! How sorry? Well, we want to introduce you to Derrick – he's the guy who thought you'd enjoy receiving Groupon emails."

Below the text is a video window of what appears to be a live webcam of Derrick, more or less dozing at his computer, along with the button Punish Derrick.

Could you resist punishing someone for filling up your Inbox with spam? Who wouldn't be curious about what the punishment might be? I clicked to punish Derrick.

With my click, one of Derrick's co-workers emerged from down the hall, argued briefly with Derrick, and then reprimanded Derrick while dousing him with a cup of hot coffee.

I had a great laugh.

A few seconds later, another message appeared: "That was pretty mean. I hope you're happy. Want to make it up to Derrick? Re-subscribe."

Not only was the Groupon unsubscribe process engaging and memorable, but it was worth talking about. It didn't take long for people to learn that Andrew Mason, the multimillionaire founder of the company, played Derrick. Andrew is a real person who doesn't take himself too seriously. As a result of Groupon's unsubscribe process, I'm writing about the company even now. Chances are some of my readers will be curious about the company and visit its website. As a result, some will ultimately become customers.

By the way, it's a good bet that 99% of your target audience has never seen this example of PIE. You could make your own entertaining version of the unsubscribe process. Punish your CEO. In social media, don't be afraid to learn from others and be a fast follower.

Rule 3: Pay It Forward

The toughest rule for social media conversations is the Pay It Forward Rule. This is the point at which most businesses' social media initiatives fail. To follow the rule, you need the answers to two questions:

1. Who composes your target audience?
2. What could you do or give that is valuable to them?

Identifying your target audience is more complex than you may imagine. Most businesses have multiple target audiences: Not just multiple *existing* customer segments with different needs and interests, but *new* prospects, potential business partners, and even employees.

The adage "Chase two rabbits, catch none" is true in social media. You must target each audience segment as narrowly and specifically as possible. Don't be overwhelmed by this: You can start with one segment and expand as you build success.

Once you've identified a target-audience segment, you must do or offer something that's valuable to that segment. Think about it. If your content is not fundamentally valuable to audience members, why will they devote their time and attention to you? They won't.

There are many ways to provide value. Being an expert in what you do, you could do any of the following:

- ❐ Alert audience members to information and trends in their area of interest or business.
- ❐ Educate audience members about things they would genuinely benefit from knowing.
- ❐ Entertain your audience (as Tom Dixon did with his Blendtec blenders or Groupon does with its unsubscribe process).
- ❐ Act as your audience's expert resource: Whenever you learn something of value, pass it along.

The goal is to entice your target-audience members to perceive you as their go-to guide in your domain of expertise.

One more reason to pay it forward in social media: Most of your prospects are not ready to buy right now. They will need your services in the future, but they don't have an interest today. You must ask yourself how you can deliver value in a way that doesn't directly relate to your products. If you can do this, you'll be top of mind when target customers realize they need you.

For example, consider Tween Brands, a billion-dollar retailer of clothing for "tween" girls. Tween Brands coined the term *tween*. If you know a girl 7–12 years old, you know a tween and you probably know the Justice brand of premium clothing.

When the team members at Tween Brands designed their first social media initiative, they needed to decide who to target. The company's studies showed that mother and daughter were equally influential in purchase decisions, a 50-50 split. Tween Brands chose to target mothers, in part because the moms have the money.

So what could Tween Brands do or give that would be valuable for moms (and no doubt some dads) who aren't necessarily in the market for girls' clothing right now? What could they do to engage these people so that Tween Brands will have moms' attention tomorrow, or next month, or next year, when the moms are interested in buying?

Tween Brands decided to focus on helping moms build their daughters' self-esteem. Tween Brands created a social media campaign that solicited success stories and propagated them through the Tween Brands Facebook page, www.facebook.com/Justice. In this forum, moms genuinely benefited from other moms' good ideas. What's more, the participating moms generated far more material than Tween Brands could have generated alone because *none of us is as smart as all of us!*

Moms were happy to participate. In fact, within a matter of months, more than 100,000 moms had joined the self-esteem campaign, and everybody was benefiting.

Tween Brands had a winning social media initiative blasting off. Lots of conversation happened among Justice employees, Justice-buying moms, and other moms. These conversations contained success stories that were personal, interesting, and educational. Because Tween Brands had created the venue for the conversations, the people behind the Justice brand were perceived as genuinely caring about the self-esteem of tweens.

It's not a huge leap from self-esteem to premium clothing. Tween Brands offered periodic coupons for 40% savings on Justice products. Although economic benefit is a powerful value proposition in its own right, it only works when you have people's attention and they are ready to buy.

Today, roughly five years later, Tween Brands' Justice strategy has evolved, presumably because the company's social media team listened to their audience and learned what the audience found to be even more compelling. Now more than 650,000 moms "like" the Justice Facebook Page. And amazingly often, these moms print the coupon offered (which has a trackable code) and head to their local malls with their daughters to shop Justice.

If your initiative is valuable to your target-audience members, they will continue to follow what you do. With the attention comes the opportunity for a relationship and trust.

Follow these three simple rules for social media dialogue:

1. The Cocktail Party Rule
2. PIE
3. The Pay It Forward Rule.

When you follow these rules, you're far more likely to connect with and retain your target audience. And that means the potential for more business.

In the next chapter, I'll discuss how to gain insights not only from those interested in your products and services, but from those who are dissatisfied with your competitors.

And in later chapters, you'll see the three rules in action. In Chapter 6, you'll discover a list of 10 things *not to do* in social media.

CHAPTER 3 SUMMARY

- ❏ Social media conversations allow you to *crowdsource,* or harvest customers' and others' ideas in an organized manner. These ideas help you to improve your products while filling your pipeline.

- ❏ Tools for crowdsourcing include idea exchanges, blogs, Facebook, Twitter, LinkedIn groups, and more.

- ❏ It's easy to find B2C applications of social media. B2B applications of social media are equally compelling but harder to find because they serve narrow target audiences.

- ❏ The dialogue you create with social media tools helps you to build relationships that increase trust. Trust is the foundation for selling. *Randy's Journal,* about Boeing, is a great example of this.

- ❏ Social media is not just for traditional push marketing. It has much wider applications.

❏ There are three important rules for using social media successfully to build business:

1. The Cocktail Party Rule (engage in two-way conversations)

2. PIE (display personality and be interesting and entertaining)

3. The Pay It Forward Rule (provide something your target audience perceives as valuable)

Because most companies neglect Rule 3, most social media initiatives fail.

CHAPTER 4

SOCIAL MEDIA PROVIDES
FAST AND TIMELY INSIDER KNOWLEDGE
FOR COMPETITIVE ADVANTAGE

Maybe you've heard the old joke about two guys hiking in the woods. They startle a grizzly bear, exactly what you're not supposed to do. Hiking in bear country in Glacier National Park, in Montana, I learned to be noisy. Noise scares away the bears; they're not interested in human confrontation.

Anyway, these guys startle the bear, so the one guy gingerly removes his backpack and pulls out his running shoes. As he's lacing up, the other guy looks at him and says, "You can't outrun a bear." The first guy replies, "Oh, I don't have to. I only have to outrun you!"

In a world of accelerating change, the key to success is not necessarily having the next big idea or over-the-top product. Oftentimes, the ability to outrun your competition, even by a little bit, can make all the difference. Social media offers tools to do just that.

Using familiar social media tools such as LinkedIn, Google, and Twitter can help you outrun your competitors – at virtually no cost. You can use these tools to do the following:

- Conduct market research
- Solicit product and service ideas from people willing to buy
- Discover competitors' vulnerabilities
- Unearth new opportunities
- Receive feedback on existing products and services

Connect to the Secret Weapon for
Getting the Information You Need to Succeed

In 2003, as CEO of the telecom software company CoManage Corporation, I found myself on a business trip to California. I was sitting in a hotel bar, reading *The Wall Street Journal* and sipping a glass of Cabernet. I was exploring the details of another stellar quarterly earnings report by eBay. According to the article, the Internet go-go days were coming back after the 2000 crash, at least for eBay.

The report got me wondering about what, precisely, made eBay so successful. I'd bought and sold products using the service, and it wasn't exactly life changing. The company's site design and user experience were at best okay.

Ultimately, I concluded that eBay success comes from one key capability: At its core, eBay is an engine that can connect two people with an obscure but shared interest in trading a specific product.

As a then 20-year telecom veteran, I started wondering about connecting people with an obscure but shared interest in trading information rather than products. What if people could connect with others to talk about their favorite sports teams, politics, religion, business, hobbies, arts, or whatever? What if the conversation could be streamed live on the Internet, recorded, and published as a podcast?

Today, the answer to those questions is a service called TalkShoe (www.TalkShoe.com). More than 700,000 podcasts have been created on the platform since 2006. Yet I nearly walked away from the idea less than one month after starting the company.

Here's the story of how TalkShoe came to be, which involved using the power of social networking on LinkedIn. To my mind, this story reveals the single best trick I've ever used in business.

Fast-forward two years from the California business trip and my original idea of connecting people who share an interest in information. In 2005, I formed PCS Corp (aka People Connection Service), doing business as TalkShoe. I hired my first employee, Aaron Brauser. (Aaron's last name is pronounced "browser" – what a great name for the first employee of an Internet company.)

Aaron is a product manager, a person who looks at the competitive landscape and the potential wants and needs of prospective customers and then creates a document that lists product requirements. Product requirements tell software engineers exactly what to build. Product management is perhaps the toughest job in the world because there are so many degrees of freedom. Aaron had worked for me before, and he's the very rare person who has the gift for doing product management effectively.

My instructions to Aaron were simple: "Do your thing" and update me at 8 a.m. every Saturday at our local Panera Bread restaurant. Unfortunately, at our fourth meeting, even before the end of TalkShoe's first month of existence, Aaron revealed that he'd discovered another company already doing exactly what we were envisioning.

That didn't bother me; in fact, it confirmed that others were seeing the same market opportunity that I was. "Aaron, it takes many companies to make a real market. That's not a bad thing," I said.

"Wait, Dave. That's not the problem," Aaron responded. "The company has been around for five years, and it's raised perhaps $50 million dollars in venture capital. I'll bet you a buck you've never heard of it: Ingenio."

Now *that* was a problem. If $50 million can't put a company on the radar screen, there must be a fatal flaw in the concept.

My next thought was to calculate the cost of two weeks' severance pay for Aaron. I have ideas all the time. If this one was a loser, well, my total investment in TalkShoe was just one month of Aaron's salary. It might be time to move on.

But I had another thought. I realized I had access to a tool that might just reveal Ingenio's fatal flaw as well as a way around it. If there wasn't a way around the flaw, I could find that out too.

The tool was the professional networking service LinkedIn (www.linkedin.com). LinkedIn is like a Google for finding people, ones who have knowledge and experience that can help your business. I'm not talking about corporate espionage or anything immoral. I'm simply talking about people who have information and/or experience they are willing to share free.

As an early user of LinkedIn, my member number is 98,323 on a service that today exceeds 300 million members. My thought was to use LinkedIn to locate and talk to some former employees of Ingenio. I could learn what the company did right – and wrong – and benefit from its five years of experience.

So here's my most valuable trick in business: LinkedIn can show you a list of people who have worked at any given company (think: your competitors). These are people who have insider insights that are unbelievably valuable. And there are a lot of these people. Experience has shown that, listed on LinkedIn, most companies have roughly twice as many former employees as current employees.

In 2005, LinkedIn was relatively small (not yet two years old) and my number of LinkedIn connections was small. Not to mention that Ingenio was a small business. Still, a brief search revealed nine former Ingenio employees. Reviewing their job titles, I selected a former executive (VP of business development) living outside the United States, and I reached out to him through a mutual LinkedIn connection (see Chapter 9 for details on finding and utilizing second-degree connections).

In my request to connect, I told "Barry" that I was an entrepreneur starting a company and that I thought he could provide me some valuable guidance. Most people are happy to help in such a situation, perhaps because I'm a potential future employer in their industry. If not, people still love to talk about what they know, to show how smart they are or simply to be helpful.

When Barry and I connected by phone, I emphasized that I was not interested in proprietary or confidential information. Instead, based on his experience, I suggested that perhaps Barry would have certain insights that could help my start-up.

After describing my idea for a service not much different from Ingenio, I asked Barry to identify what he thought my biggest challenges would be. He said "Dave, think of it like this: You will have a customer acquisition cost, call it x. You will derive revenue from the customers, call it y. Initially, y will be less than x and you'll be in the hole. Now these customers won't need your service the next day, and they'll tend to forget about you. To reacquire them or to acquire replacements, you'll spend x ... to get revenue y. You see the problem?"

I relayed Barry's observations to Aaron and asked him how he thought we could stay connected with new customers without incurring reconnection cost x. Aaron had three ideas that we baked into the initial design of the service.

Seven years later, TalkShoe is a profitable company serving between one and two million monthly listeners, all because Barry told me what my start-up's big challenge would be two years before I would have actually encountered it. Isn't that the perfect time to address a problem?

LINKEDIN IS A POWERHOUSE TOOL
FOR LEARNING ABOUT ANY INDUSTRY

While we're talking about LinkedIn, I've discovered a great way to learn about any industry: using LinkedIn groups. I do this every time I land a client in an industry that I've not served before.

For example, when I signed a new client in the digital printing business, I joined the Digital Printing Group in LinkedIn. (You'll learn how to do this in Chapter 9.) Not only does the Digital Printing Group have more than 38,000 members, there are also subgroups for specialties, including wide-format printing, label printing, and such. In the main group alone, there are 250 discussions going on right now – discussions about the important issues and opportunities of the day.

By reviewing these discussion threads, you can learn about the industry at a hyper-accelerated rate. In essence, you're learning from 38,000 brains rather than just your own. (Remember, *none of us is as smart as all of us.*)

Your first reaction may be to think, "Who's got that kind of time?" Indeed, we're all incredibly busy, and tomorrow has only 24 hours, same as today. I believe that most people (including ourselves, if we're being honest) waste a material amount of time doing the wrong things because they lack the right information. LinkedIn groups, like many other social media tools, help us rapidly discover the right information through collective experience. Who doesn't have time for that?

In addition to reviewing the discussions among LinkedIn group members, you can post questions and get answers directly from experienced industry experts. What do you need to know? If you're thinking about offering a new product or service, ask experts for their input before making your investment. If you're wondering about changing the way you support customers, ask for opinions before potentially making a mistake in the market.

There are a variety of other ways to benefit from LinkedIn groups. If you're running a nonprofit organization and want to learn how to use social media most effectively, why not join the LinkedIn group called Social Media Today and post this question: "Does anyone have best-practice examples of how nonprofits are using social media?" In fact, someone already posted this question, and there are more than 300 answers ready for your review. I am especially impressed with the social media strategy of the American Red Cross.

USE SOCIAL MEDIA TO PICK OFF PROSPECTS
WHO ARE DISSATISFIED WITH YOUR COMPETITORS

The week before Christmas in 2012, Gary Hirsch, the head of a Vistage group of business executives in Tucson, Arizona, wanted to give his team members a gift. Instead of giving them something tangible, he decided to donate, on behalf of his team, selected farm animals and tools to people in the Third World.

Hirsch had heard of an organization called Heifer International that provided a service to do this. He googled the organization and discovered disturbing employee comments on Glassdoor (www.Glassdoor.com), including the following:

- ☐ Former employee: "Honest communications and, unfortunately, even ethical behavior are seriously lacking. The organization has not always been completely straightforward with its donors about how their donations are being used."

- ☐ Current employee: "Go back to the basic foundation and principles which Dan West used to initially grow the organization!"

Hirsch did some further googling and discovered a "competitor" of Heifer International's, Oxfam America. Oxfam appeared to be more highly regarded by current and former employees (on Glassdoor, 4.2 stars for Oxfam America vs. 2.7 stars for Heifer). So that's where Hirsch made his investment.

In presenting his gift, Hirsch told the group this whole story. I loved the idea of such a selfless gift at Christmastime, so on behalf of family members I purchased a menagerie of animals, including a goat, two baby goats, a pig, and several dozen chicks – not through Heifer, but through Oxfam.

Social media is an accelerator of sorts. It helps *great* organizations succeed more quickly. It helps *poor* organizations – well, you know.

You don't even have to make the effort to google a company or competitor to get the information you need. Google and Twitter offer services to monitor what people are saying about your competitors in real time. If someone complains about your competition in a tweet, blog post, review site, discussion forum, Facebook page, or almost anywhere else online, Google and Twitter will notify you. These services are free and take just a few minutes to configure. (You can get started at www.Google.com/alerts and https://twitter.com/twittersearch or learn more in Chapter 8.)

Google Alerts and Twitter Search are your running shoes for outpacing the bear relative to your competition. The services will notify you anytime someone mentions competitors. Monitor these mentions for complaints and problems, and then select the lucky salesperson of the day, the person who will reach out to each new prospect.

Your lucky salesperson is likely to hear something to this effect: "I'm so glad you called today. It's almost like you have ESP." Indeed, you've contacted prospects in the exact moment of dissatisfaction, when they are most open to potential change.

USE SOCIAL MEDIA TO
TALK CONSTANTLY TO YOUR CUSTOMERS

You can use Google Alerts and Twitter Search to receive notifications when anyone talks about *you* online. Use this information to deal with complaints, improve your products, and take advantage of hot trends. But these services are just two of the tools available to you to conduct ongoing conversations with the people who matter most to your bottom line.

Perhaps my favorite book about a business leader who's fully embraced social media in building his business is *Crush It,* by Gary Vaynerchuk. The audio version, read by the author, (available at www.Audible.com) is even better. Gary constantly goes off script. That is the most fascinating part.

I've traveled the same social path as Vaynerchuk in my role as TalkShoe CEO, and embracing social media tools helped me understand my customers better than most business leaders in the world, save for people like Gary Vaynerchuk.

While running TalkShoe, every other Thursday I'd fire up a live podcast (eating my own dog food as it were) to actually talk with those customers who wanted to connect directly with me. I did this for years until I discovered professional speaking and left TalkShoe to travel the world, spreading the gospel about the power of social media (including TalkShoe) directly to business executives. Since then I've spoken to more than 400 groups representing more than 10,000 companies in the United States, Canada, the United Kingdom, and beyond. Today, I'm working on my next start-up and putting these tools into practice once again, as TalkShoe continues to prosper under the leadership of a strong, investor-led management team.

So what is a live podcast? It's a glorified teleconference, to which people can call in via phone or computer or listen live via audio stream. They can also text-chat their comments and questions. After the teleconference, people can access a recording of the podcast by using iTunes and other services. If you've ever been on a business conference call, a WebEx call, or a GoToMeeting webinar, you understand TalkShoe, more or less.

So twice a month, I'd go live on TalkShoe and share a short update about service features, problems, whatever, with literally all of my customers who cared to connect. And then for the rest of the hour, I'd field every question, every compliment, every criticism, and every suggestion customers cared to make. Can you think of a better way to really get to know your customers?

In practice, roughly 95% of my participating customers would listen to the recording after the fact and follow up via email if they had questions or suggestions. In either mode, the experience was incredibly bonding on both sides.

This live podcasting process increased my understanding of what was important to my customers. It was market research straight from the horse's mouth. As such, it helped my company deliver better products and services. So I ask again, how well do you really know your customers?

If you are not using social media to get to know your customers and to let them get to know you, you're missing an opportunity. Visit www.TalkShoe.com to start a direct dialogue with your customers via live podcasting. You'll get valuable feedback on your products and services. This is also a great way to get new product and service ideas. Or you can set up an idea exchange (discussed in Chapter 3) or launch GetSatisfaction (covered in Chapter 15). Whatever tool you choose, start a dialogue and begin outrunning those competitors!

USE SOCIAL MEDIA TO
ALLOW NEW OPPORTUNITIES TO COME TO YOU

Social media is all about dialogue, about building trust and bi-directional learning. At the same time, however, social media offers research and business development tools that are like nothing that came before. Some of the most powerful are Google Alerts and Twitter Search.

One of my clients, Harvard Maintenance, provides janitorial services to universities and hospitals throughout the United States. The company set up a Google Alert on the phrase "janitorial RFP." (RFP stands for request for proposal.) Anytime anyone anywhere on the Web posts a request for such services, Google notifies Harvard Maintenance. Business opportunities knock on the company's front door.

A chiropractor friend of mine monitors search.Twitter.com for mentions of *"Back pain" near:15222 within:50mi.* Whenever someone mentions back pain (or headache, fibromyalgia, etc.) in his vicinity, he discovers another hot prospect.

What do people mention when they are interested in what your company offers? Ask your clients and friends what they would google to find answers to the problems your business solves. Set up alerts and searches, and let the business come to you.

Understand Why This Matters

Social media and social networking tools are part of an evolving communication continuum that started out with hieroglyphs and smoke signals and continued with telegrams, faxes, pagers, and email. The continuum has now progressed to Facebook, Google+, Pinterest, Yammer, SnapChat, Instagram, Vine, MeMeMe, and the like (I made up that last one ;-). If you want to compete in today's marketplace, you have to continue to evolve with the communication continuum.

For example, imagine that, while you are out of town on a business trip, your mobile phone dies. Cut off from your professional world, you have no idea what's happening back at the ranch. When you return to the office, it turns out that everybody's mobile devices are down ... not worldwide, just at your company. You are one generation behind in communication technology. You feel the gap, and it's not a fun place to be, given intense competition and a tough economy.

Here's the reality: If your competition figures out how to apply these social tools before you do, you'll be one generation behind in communication technology. You may not feel the gap immediately, but it will be there – at a tremendous cost to your business.

Sticking with the tried and true is a recipe for disaster in a world of accelerating change. It's time to adopt the most useful of these new information-advantage tools to apply new competitive strategies, so that the bear is feasting on your competition instead of on you. Social media provides ample tools to discover the vulnerabilities of your competitors, opportunities for new customers, and feedback from existing customers.

In the next chapter, I'll explain how to capture, organize, and share this information so that your new employees get up to speed faster, your current employees work smarter, and your departing employees subtract less organizational knowledge as they move on.

LinkedIn Advanced People Search Is Free

You can connect with your competitors' former employees by signing in to LinkedIn and clicking on the Advanced button, next to the People Search box in the upper-right screen area.

You'll see a dozen different attributes that you can use to search for people. Specify the company name of your key competitors, set the drop-down menu to past employees, and prepare to be amazed. I don't know of any other tool in the world that can show you information this important.

I call this LinkedIn Advanced People Search trick Insider Insights. It's the most valuable tool I've ever discovered for obtaining strategic competitive information. If you're not doing this, just imagine how it will hurt your business if your competitors are doing it. Best to get there first.

CHAPTER 4 SUMMARY

❑ Social media provides fast and timely insider knowledge that offers a competitive advantage.

❑ LinkedIn makes it easy for you to talk to (and learn from) your competitors' former employees. LinkedIn's Advanced People Search allows you to use a dozen different attributes to search for people. The service is free.

❑ You can learn about any industry (including yours and your customers') by participating in an appropriate LinkedIn group. Again, the service is free.

❑ Social media allows you to discover virtually anything, including people complaining about your competitors (aka new opportunities). When you use Google Alerts and Twitter Search, you don't even have to search for the information; it comes to you.

❑ You can use social media tools (including my company TalkShoe) to talk to your customers en masse. Direct feedback about your products and services will equip your team with the information required to improve your company's competitiveness.

❑ If your competition figures out how to apply these social tools before you do, you'll be one generation behind in communication technology. You may not feel the gap immediately, but it will be there – at a tremendous cost to your business.

CHAPTER 5

USE SOCIAL MEDIA TO SHARE AND PRESERVE KNOWLEDGE WHILE INCREASING EFFICIENCY

When I started the interactive podcasting service called TalkShoe.com in 2005, I hired a team of people who knew more about social media than 99.9% of businesspeople on the planet, then or now.

Today, I can't tell you which team member came up with this next idea, but my best guess is that it was our IT manager, Peter. In any case, Peter was definitely involved in implementing it.

As head of IT, Peter was always working to improve information management and communication within the company. So in early 2006, he set up a wiki (as in *Wikipedia*) for our employees to use.

You're probably familiar with Wikipedia, the user-generated encyclopedia of human knowledge. It is now the seventh-most-trafficked website on the Internet. Even if you've never visited directly, you've likely seen Wikipedia entries among the top search results after a Google search.

Peter was likely thinking, "What if we could build a 'Wikipedia' not of all human knowledge, but of all corporate knowledge?" Since the software was (and still is) available free from TWiki (www.TWiki.org), Peter decided to try an experiment.

After installing the TWiki software on our servers, Peter set up a section for each department in the company: Management, Human Resources (HR), Marketing, Sales, Customer Support, etc.

Then Peter asked other employees to stop emailing documents, presentations, and spreadsheets within the company. Instead, he asked us to post these files on our "corporate Wikipedia" and then send links to the documents via email.

The results were stunning. Most noticeably, internal email dropped dramatically. In hindsight, it's obvious why: So much of corporate email is related to Microsoft Office documents being sent back and forth between employees like a game of corporate ping-pong. On a TWiki, employees can comment and edit collaboratively, with version changes tracked automatically (just as people collaborate on Wikipedia).

Less obvious but equally profound, employees now know exactly where to get the latest information about any project in the company. Want the current schedule for the next software release? No need to email the product manager. Just check the TWiki. Need the newest PowerPoint presentation on our various products? No need to email the Marketing Department and wait for a response. Just check the TWiki.

As powerful as the savings that come from decreased email ping-pong are, the greatest benefits come from something else.

Survive (and Prosper) Through Inevitable Employee Turnover

According to the U.S. Department of Labor, the average employee now entering the workforce will have 10–14 jobs – *by the time he or she is 38 years old!* That means as employers we have employees for an average of about 18 months. How do we get them up to speed faster and preserve more of their corporate contribution when they leave? Again, the answer is TWiki. Here is an example.

TalkShoe had roughly a dozen employees. In addition to my roles as founder and CEO, I was in charge of HR. As soon as I understood what TWiki could do, I took control of the HR section of the site. I implemented our entire onboarding process right there.

When the next new employee joined TalkShoe, I was ready with, "Welcome to TalkShoe. Here's your computer, username, and password. Access our TWiki at this Web address and get yourself onboard. See you in a few hours."

The new employee signed on and discovered the I-9, W-4, and Employment Agreement forms, with instructions to complete, print, and sign, as I wanted hard copies for our personnel files (and the IRS).

Each new employee also found the employee handbook, holiday schedule, etc., on the TWiki. After completing the HR process, the employee would access the branch of the TWiki corresponding to his or her job function, most often in software engineering. There the employee would find all relevant product and project documentation, from the beginning of a project to the current day. As such, new employees came up to speed much faster than before.

The TWiki was useful when employees resigned. (The few resignations we had tended to be incredibly painful to me.) In such cases, typically given two weeks' notice, I'd ask the employee to use his or her remaining time to ensure that absolutely everything of potential team or archival value was posted to the relevant sections of the TWiki. Like Wikipedia, TWiki contains a powerful search function, not to mention change tracking and hyperlinking among documents. Because of this, such information would benefit the organization in ways unanticipated – weeks, months, and even years later.

Compare this to how most companies operate. In some cases companies do not provide new employees with access to important information, or the new employees are mentored by individuals whose own productivity is negatively affected, even as the process takes longer and is less effective than TWiki onboarding. When employees leave the organization, their computers (including the extensive email collection) are wiped clean for the next person to use, deleting an entire archive of valuable corporate information. This practice makes sense only because, typically, no one else can decode the former employee's personal filing system, let along benefit from his or her historical email cache.

Learn to Overcome the Tyranny of Email

According to John Freeman's book, *The Tyranny of Email – The 4,000-Year Journey to Your Inbox,* in corporate America we are now spending more than 40% of our time working email. The vehicle is at best an inefficient method of communicating. It's overrun with spam, replies to all, and BCCs, not to mention that roughly 6 out of every 10 messages are irrelevant to us. Although we can't do much about the outside world, we can certainly do better internally.

Unlike a phone call or text message, email is an asynchronous rather than instantaneous communication vehicle. The biggest mistake we are collectively making with email is using it for sharing time-critical information. In so doing, we're mixing this information with everything else, thereby making us slaves to our Inboxes. Every time your Blackberry/Android/iPhone goes "bing," you have to check it in case the message is a time-critical message.

Much criticism has been leveled at members of Generation Y for the way they communicate, but here's one place where we can look to them for guidance. While they use electronic communication far more often than older generations, virtually none of it is email. Interesting.

Instead, when sending time-critical information, members of Gen Y send a text. Otherwise, they use a rich information medium (chat, audio, video, photos, discussions, etc.) called Facebook. *In corporate America, we should be using the same strategy, although not the same tools.*

Specifically, when sending time-critical information among employees, we should use texting or Yammer (discussed in Chapter 2). For everything else internally, we should use TWiki or Ning, the latter being a kind of *corporate* Facebook. We'll explore Ning in detail in Chapter 17. We should look to email only for external communication and the rare internal message that has minimal group value.

Companies following this strategy are reporting dramatic gains in organizational learning. They're getting employees up to speed faster when they join, and they're preserving more organizational knowledge when they depart.

UNLIKE THE ROLLING STONES, YOU CAN GETSATISFACTION

Every few years a company emerges by establishing its brand and achieving undying customer loyalty by providing unbelievable customer service. If you've ever dealt with Nordstrom, you know the experience. Others in this lofty category include L.L. Bean, Four Seasons Hotels and Resorts, Apple, Starbucks, and Lexus. And, of course, Zappos.

Zappos (www.zappos.com) is an Internet retailer that sells shoes. If you think about it, the one thing that should be all but impossible to sell on the Internet is shoes. Have you ever purchased shoes without testing the fit? Typically, I try on many pairs before making a selection. (Having wide feet sucks, although I can float upside-down in a swimming pool.)

To solve this problem, Zappos adopted an insane customer service approach. No matter what you buy, shipping is always free (no minimum). So is return shipping. No questions asked; no hassles ever.

You can, for example, order three different sizes of a given shoe and keep just the pair that fits best. You have up to 365 days to return the other two pairs. You can even return all three pairs.

If by chance you purchase something on February 29 (Leap Day), you have until the next Leap Day to return it.

That's an unbelievable four years, and sometimes eight. As I said, it's insane.

Zappos' CEO, Tony Hseih, recently revealed a key component of the company formula. It's something that 70,000 other businesses are now doing to improve their own customer service. Your business can too.

Zappos' not-so-secret weapon is a cloud-based community called GetSatisfaction (https://getsatisfaction.com/corp/), or GetSat. This social media software allows you to create a community consisting of customers and your support personnel. In short, it's a new social media form of the traditional customer support forum. But it's more than that. GetSat is the ultimate embodiment of "the wisdom of crowds" meets "knowledge capture and reuse." According to Hseih:

> There's a simple reason that we were one of the first to raise our hands at Zappos and start using GetSatisfaction: A lot of our approach to making people happy with timely, human customer service is already baked into this product. They get it.

GetSat gives your customers the opportunity to type a question in normal language syntax; the software then suggests possible matching questions for which it already has answers. Although you can see the advantage in that, it gets better. If the user doesn't find a relevant question and answer, he or she can post the question for other customers to answer. And they often do.

People like to share what they know, to show that they're smart or to be helpful. Either way, they often answer support questions before your Support Team does. Your team simply reviews the proposed answers and approves, rejects, or edits them for accuracy. Thus, customers and your Support Team share answers, ideas, and solutions. This decreases the load on your Support Team. More important, you get the synergy of *none of us is as smart as all of us.*

TalkShoe started using GetSat in 2008. Consider the compelling value proposition that GetSat offers. Companies that use GetSat report, on average:

❑ An 89% reduction in customer support load. That's roughly a tenfold gain!

❑ Increased sense of customer community. After all, the happiest, most knowledgeable fellow customers are the ones who participate.

❑ Improved customer satisfaction scores.

What's not to love? You can reduce costs and get better results by following the same template for customer service excellence that Zappos uses.

At the time of this writing, the small-business version of GetSat starts at $1,200/month. This is likely to yield the single best return on investment (ROI) you've ever achieved in business. At TalkShoe it certainly did.

GetSat is an example of how a social media tool can actually save you more time than it requires – while improving results.

WHERE WILL YOU BEGIN TO TAKE ACTION?

Having read this far, I hope you are convinced that social media has the power to transform your business and help you beat your competition. At the same time, you've now encountered more ideas than you can possibly implement in the next few months – maybe even in the next few years. The good news is that you don't have to do it all to succeed in social media. In fact, it's better to do a few things well than many things not so well.

Start on the right foot by reading Chapter 6, which explains 10 things *not* to do with social media. Then, if you are a reader who appreciates the benefits of planning, read Chapter 7. This chapter outlines 11 steps to developing a successful social media plan. It will walk you through the process of figuring out which tools make sense for your business as well as how to create a plan for implementation.

Each of Chapters 8–17 explores a specific social media service, describing that tool's applications and advantages, and provides plenty of examples. You'll find chapters on LinkedIn, Facebook, Ning, Google+, podcasting, and more. Consider each tool in light of the social media plan you develop.

Chapters 18–23 take you beyond specific tools to consider how to use social media in effective and strategic ways. Chapter 18 unveils the power of customer testimonials. Read Chapter 19 to discover how to use an RSS dashboard to reduce information overload. Read Chapter 20 to learn to stop fearing your critics and use them to advantage. Chapter 21 shows you, step-by-step, how to decide if the next new hot service is for you (or if you can happily ignore it). Chapter 22 provides a blueprint for true social media success: converting visitors, Likers, and followers to customers. Chapter 23 wraps things up and issues your call to action.

I recognize that some readers would rather experiment than plan. I encourage these readers to think about Chapters 8–17 as a restaurant menu. When you walk into a restaurant, you may see 50 items on the menu. No matter how many of the offerings capture your attention, you don't say to your server, "Bring me one of each."

Instead, you choose the one or two items that look promising and order those. You may return another day and order something else, sampling many of the restaurant offerings over time.

Social media tools are a lot like a Chinese restaurant, except that most cost nothing or can at least be tried free. Pick one that looks promising and try it out. Later, you can try the next most attractive option. As in any aspect of business, it's better to do one thing well than several things poorly.

I recommend chartering a small team of volunteers – not draftees – to pilot a social media application at your company. If the initiative yields process improvements, accelerated learning, increased revenues, or other positive returns, scale it up to the rest of the organization. If the initiative doesn't work out, fail fast and try the next one.

First, get some critical information under your belt. Read Chapter 6 to learn what not to do in social media.

CHAPTER 5 SUMMARY

- ❏ Capturing and sharing organizational knowledge is more important than ever. The U.S. Department of Labor predicts that the average employee now entering the workforce will have 10–14 jobs – *by the time he or she is 38!*

- ❏ According to John Freeman's book, *The Tyranny of Email – The 4,000-Year Journey to Your Inbox,* we, as members of corporate America, spend more than 40% of our time on email during the business day. Tools that are more efficient are readily available.

- ❏ Implementing your own "business Wikipedia," using tools from TWiki, allows you to share and preserve knowledge while reducing time spent on email.

- ❏ TWiki can be an example of how a social media tool can actually save more time than it requires. And improve results.

- ❏ Any company can follow the Zappos template for excellent customer service. Zappos' not-so-secret tool, GetSatisfaction, is available to any business.

CHAPTER 6

TEN SOCIAL MEDIA MISTAKES: DON'T DO THIS IN THE OFFICE

A recent study by the Chicago-based firm Slack Barshinger showed that the majority of small and medium-sized businesses are now "heavily involved with social media, with about half using blogs, wikis (content collaboration software), Twitter, or other social media channels for business purposes."

If your company and team are not yet engaged, it's time to jump in before your competitors beat you to the punch. And "punch" is an appropriate term.

Social media marketing is not your father's marketing. When participating in social media, here are 10 basic rules about what *not* to do:

1. Don't get started in social media if you have significant product weaknesses or customer support issues. Engaging in social media makes good businesses more successful and bad businesses bankrupt. But don't delay for long; address the issues and then jump in.

2. Don't use social media to market or sell explicitly. Instead, educate, enlighten, inform, and entertain your audience. In so doing, you'll position yourself and your company as experts in your field and benefit from a media halo.

3. Don't "set it and forget it." Lack of conversation makes you look worse than not showing up at all. Once started, sustain your participation and interaction. Remember the Cocktail Party Rule from

Chapter 3: Once you introduce yourself, be prepared to participate in the resulting conversation.

4. Don't go negative. Emphasize your strengths and
   advantages rather than pointing to a competitor's
   weaknesses. And never, never, *never* criticize your
   critics. Thank them for their input and do your best
   to address their issues. Even if you can't make your
   critics happy, you'll demonstrate to everyone else
   that your company is tuned in and responsive to its
   customers.

5. Don't mix personal and business accounts, personas, etc. In fact, please make sure that your company owns your social media accounts. There are
   endless stories about employees who used their
   personal Facebook (or Twitter, etc.) account for
   business. After the employee departs, the company
   may not be able to access that account. Indeed, the
   company may have no ownership claim at all.

6. Don't expect to control the conversation fully. Social media is not an advertisement, product brochure, newsletter, email blast, or one-way monologue; it's a conversation. Conversations are bidirectional and can have rough edges. Even if you
   don't want to participate, your customers and prospects are already talking. Join them.

7. Don't worry about some negativity. Studies show
   that a little negativity increases credibility and em-
   pathy. Paraphrasing Abraham Lincoln, "You can't
   please all of the people all of the time." Be responsive to the negative, but know that such information can help people figure out under what cir-
   cumstances they should *not* be your customers. In
   one study, management at Petco found that prod-
   uct-return rates fell by 45% after Petco.com ena-
   bled customer reviews.

8. Don't feel the need to talk about everything. I like sausage, but I don't want to see it made. Be honest *and* use discretion. Authenticity is one thing; opening the kimono is something else.

9. Don't be a generalist. With literally hundreds of millions of blogs, videos, podcasts, tweets, etc., to choose from, every individual can tailor content consumption to his or her exact interests. Focus on one topic and do it well. As a rule, in a world of information overload, the narrower your focus, the better.

10. Don't overwhelm your followers with information that is too much or too frequent. Everybody has a busy life and nobody enjoys "Twitter-rhea." Providing too much information is as bad as providing too little. In either case, your audience will disconnect. For your social media, find the "Goldilocks Zone" based on your audience's appetite for your information. This allows you to focus on content that offers the highest value.

Social media is now "table stakes" for interacting with your customers, partners, suppliers, and even employees. By getting started today, your company can (to borrow an idea from Charles Darwin) adapt to a changing environment more quickly than your competitors – to survive and even prosper. Now is the time; what are you waiting for?

Chapter 6 Summary

Social media marketing is not your father's marketing. Here are basic rules about what *not* to do, when participating in social media:

- ❏ Don't get started in social media if you have significant product weaknesses or customer support issues.

- ❏ Don't use social media to explicitly market or sell.

- ❏ Don't "set it and forget it."

- ❏ Don't go negative about competitors or critics.

- ❏ Don't mix personal and business accounts, personas, etc.

- ❏ Don't expect to control the conversation fully.

- ❏ Don't worry about some negativity.

- ❏ Don't feel the need to talk about everything.

- ❏ Don't be a generalist.

- ❏ Don't overwhelm your followers with information that is too much or too frequent.

CHAPTER 7

WORK SMART:
DEVELOP A SUCCESSFUL SOCIAL MEDIA PLAN

Social media has the power to transform your business. At the same time, it's possible to spend a lot of time and energy on social media without getting results. Your opportunity to capitalize on the power of social media increases dramatically when you develop a coherent social media plan.

In this chapter, I'll recommend a step-by-step approach for developing a social media plan that works well for your specific situation. First, however, I'll summarize a few of the key concepts and benefits we've explored so far:

1. SOCIAL NETWORKING ALLOWS YOU TO EXPAND YOUR KNOWLEDGE EXPONENTIALLY

You've seen that *none of us is as smart as all of us.* A particularly striking illustration is the Twitter conversation that occurred on the night Osama Bin Laden was killed.

You've learned that social media tools accelerate learning by inviting input from a wide range of stakeholders, all of whom are willing to give you their ideas and share their expertise (think LinkedIn and an idea exchange). Social media also allows you to create forums in which people can build on each other's ideas, creating synergies and developing solutions well beyond the capacity of any individual (think Yammer).

2. SOCIAL NETWORKING PROVIDES BIDIRECTIONAL
    LEARNING, GIVING DOUBLE RETURN ON YOUR EFFORTS

    Social media invites current and potential customers to
    tell you how to improve products and services. At the
    same time these people are giving you priceless infor-
    mation, they are learning about your company and what
    you have to offer (think the Boeing-related blog posts of
    Randy's Journal).

3. SOCIAL NETWORKING HELPS FILL YOUR PIPELINE

    People who engage with you in social media are not nec-
    essarily ready to buy. However, your continuing conver-
    sation keeps you top of mind. When people in your net-
    work are ready to buy, they will already know you, trust
    you, and be informed about your offerings. Assuming you
    are providing value to your target audience, that audience,
    and your pipeline, will continue to grow (think Tween
    Brands' Facebook campaign to promote the Justice
    brand).

4. SOCIAL MEDIA HELPS YOU
    OUTRUN YOUR COMPETITION

    Social media tools give you access to industry experts and
    competitors' former employees – two groups that have
    and are willing to share invaluable information. Social
    media tools also allow you to find and contact prospects
    when they express dissatisfaction with your competitors.
    The tools allow you to create situations in which new op-
    portunities come to you (think Google Alerts and Twitter
    Search). The tools allow you to get up to speed quickly on
    any industry by reviewing and participating in specialized
    discussions (think LinkedIn groups).

5. SOCIAL NETWORKING CAN
    SAVE TIME AND INCREASE EFFICIENCY

    Social media tools allow you to capture and access
    knowledge, eliminating the constant need to send and
    search email. The savings in time and reduced frustration

make a substantial difference in efficiency. What's more, these tools allow you to capture and easily access knowledge that typically is locked in employees' and customers' heads. This allows employees and customers to build on each other's knowledge (think internal TWiki and GetSatisfaction).

In virtually any business, faster learning and expanded connections lead to increased revenues. That's what's in it for us – but remember that social media initiatives work only if they first provide value to the target audience. Social media is not about us; it's about them.

The typical social campaign requires a larger investment of time than money. Nonetheless, such initiatives can save more time than they consume by improving customer support, product management, and internal communication processes – for example, by substantially reducing email.

In a social media world, information flows freely. Prospects learn, from your existing customers and your competitors' customers, about the realities of your respective products and services.

In a world of "complete information," not everyone will survive. Now is the time to address any weaknesses in your products, services, and customer support policies. Now is the time to improve even your corporate culture and your hiring and firing processes. (These are topics of conversation in social media. See posted conversations, if you need some tips about where to start.)

Social tools are too powerful to ignore. You must learn how to apply them before your competitors do.

FOLLOW 11 STEPS TO SUCCESS

It's not atypical for company executives to decide to launch a Facebook page or begin tweeting because they've seen other companies do so successfully. However, *selecting tools should actually be the sixth step in your process, not the first.*

Below are 11 straightforward steps to designing a social media initiative. Follow these steps to increases your initiative's probability of success. These steps apply to both B2C and B2B initiatives. I recommend documenting each step in writing. Create a two- or three-page plan that informs everyone on your team of your strategy and your tactics.

Step 1   Define Objective(s) and Conversion Steps

Step 2   Analyze the Competition

Step 3   Identify and Segment the Target
          Audience(s)

Step 4   Select Keywords

Step 5   Create a Compelling Value Proposition for
          the Target Audience

Step 6   Commit to Specific Tools and Budget

Step 7   Ensure Accountability

Step 8   Define Engagement Metrics

Step 9   Create Content

Step 10   Develop a Promotion Plan

Step 11   Measure Results

Keep in mind that social media is just one component of your marketing plan. Remember to keep investing in your website, product information, customer forums, trade shows, email marketing, public relations, and other proven tools that compose an integrated marketing strategy. In a world of mouth, each component has a role, even as the resource allocations shift among tools.

One final key point before we look at the 11 steps for achieving social media success. There are actually two major tasks in making social media work for your business. Fail on either one and you've got nothing.

First, you must *engage* audience members. To do so, your initiative must have compelling and continuous value for them, and they must be aware of it. In short, you must attract and retain their attention.

Second, you must *convert* a relevant percentage of your audience to prospects, customers, advocates, or helpers – a percentage that allows you to realize business benefits. Otherwise, a Facebook Like or a Twitter follower has little to no value.

Here is the only winning formula: Engage ... then convert!

Step 1: Define Objective(s) and Conversion Steps

As you consider your objectives, think of your website and associated social initiatives as a dynamic, rather than a static, advertisement of your products and services. Your digital presence is *not* an online product brochure. Instead, it should be a *conversion engine* designed to convert people from visitors to customers. Social initiatives aid this cause because they are more engaging than traditional websites.

Start by writing down your objectives and making them specific, measurable, and time-bound. For example, you may be aiming to increase revenues of the XYZ product line by 12% in the next year. Fine, but that's too big to be actionable. In this case, define the sub-objectives (aka conversion steps) that lead to the goal, For example, sub-objectives could be to

- ☐ Increase unique website visitors by 30%
- ☐ While sustaining a 3% purchase rate (aka conversions)
- ☐ At a transaction value 33% above average
- ☐ Resulting in a 12% increase in revenues ($30\% \times 3\% \times 133\% = 12\%$)

The next level of granularity involves identifying components that contribute to unique website visitors, and so on.

Only the rare visitor lands on your home page or blog and becomes a customer in the next step. Typically, a visitor takes a series of conversion steps along the way. Signing up for your email newsletter makes him or her more likely to become a customer ultimately, because your company is more frequently top of mind. Downloading a white paper allows the visitor to understand your expertise and frames thinking in a way that increases the likelihood of purchase. So does clicking on a button that says "Have a salesperson contact me."

Take time to think about the steps that visitors to your website, blog, Facebook page, etc. must take to become your customers. Yes, this is a hard question. However, if you can map them, you can measure them, and then you can improve your effectiveness at achieving them. What would it mean if you could achieve a higher conversion rate, even with the same number of visitors?

While by no means an exhaustive list, potential conversion steps for your company may include

- Viewing a specific website page or landing page
- Moving from a given website page (or blog post, etc.) from your company to another page from your company
- Signing up for your email marketing program
- Clicking on Like, Follow, or Subscribe (See Chapter 19, about RSS.)
- Downloading a white paper
- Clicking on an option to chat online
- Clicking on the button "Have a salesperson contact me"
- Clicking on the Buy button

Step 2: Analyze the Competition

As the starting point in designing any social media initiative, learn from the experience of others. Although examples in this book will be instructive, in many cases you can learn more about what works in your industry by reviewing the successes and failures of your competitors.

Perhaps the best way to know who's winning or losing is to review website traffic data, measured in terms of unique monthly visitors. This data is available free at Compete (www.compete.com) and SEMrush[4] (www.semrush.com). To analyze the website traffic of a competitor, enter the competitor's Web address and then review the resulting traffic graphs. Note both the absolute number of visitors in the latest month and the traffic trend (up, down, or flat) over time. Repeat the process to learn about other competitors' traffic statistics.

Note those competitors doing best (and perhaps worst), and visit their websites to review their social initiatives (Facebook, Twitter, YouTube, blog, Google+, etc.). These are typically accessible directly from a homepage. Evaluate what each competitor is doing right and wrong, and use what you learn to guide your own initiatives.

Step 3: Identify and Segment the Target Audience(s)

Identifying and detailing your target audience(s) are key to serving the audience(s). Social media allows you to pursue more narrowly defined audiences than previous marketing and advertising media allowed. The more specifically you can define and segment your target audiences, the more effectively you can serve them.

---

[4] SEM: Search engine marketing

After you've delineated your target audiences, select those that are most important to your company. In social media, it's more important to be fully engaged in a few places than to touch everything lightly.

Pick those audiences that are most valuable to you, balancing their potential importance with the resources required to engage them fully. As the saying goes: Chase two rabbits, catch none.

Step 4: Select Keywords

Half of all Internet traffic starts with a search. The key question is this: What words or phrases are your prospects using when they've never heard of you but they're looking for information about what you do? Google's Ad-Words Keyword Planner tool can answer this question. The tool provides a fascinating glimpse into human search psychology.

Access the AdWords Keyword Planner by visiting https://adwords.google.com/KeywordPlanner or by scanning the QR code that follows.

Scan for Google's keyword-planning tool

For many companies, just a dozen key phrases can represent a meaningful volume of potential search impressions. The goal is to "own" these phrases, ideally resulting in an organic (i.e., naturally occurring as opposed to paid) ranking on page 1 of Google search results. If you pursue too many keywords, you'll dilute your efforts and likely be successful with none.

Imagine for a moment that you focus on just a single keyword phrase. (In my case, it might be *social media consultant*.) Imagine that you add a compelling blog post about that topic *every week* or add a new landing page to your website about that topic, or post in a relevant LinkedIn group about that topic, or post on Google+ about that topic. It's not hard to believe that in time Google will start ranking your content higher in Google search results for that keyword phrase.

On the other hand, imagine that you select 104 keywords and, still posting weekly, rotate sequentially through every one so that each keyword phrase is featured in a post once every two years (across 104 weeks). It's unlikely that any of your phrases will be anything but obscure on Google.

Clicks on organic results (the ones you can't buy but must earn by posting valuable, relevant content) are free and represent 77% of all clicks on Google. I have nothing against pay-per-click if it generates a positive ROI, but organic is the bigger game.

The key to achieving optimal organic ranking for a given phrase is to use the phrase consistently in relevant social and Web content. Specifically, use it in the titles, URLs (Universal Resource Locators, aka web page addresses), and first 100 words of content on your website, in your blog, on Facebook, in LinkedIn, and everywhere else.

This bears repeating. To achieve optimal organic ranking for a given phrase, use it consistently in relevant social and Web content. Specifically, use it in

- ☐ Page and content titles
- ☐ URLs
- ☐ First 100 words of content

At the time of this writing, Google has approximately two-thirds of the search market, and Google will change algorithms 500 times in the next 12 months. The only way to win the search game is to produce content *regularly* that is *relevant* to your target audience, *consistently* using your *relevant keywords* in your content.

Step 5: Create a Compelling Value Proposition for the Target Audience

This is the most important of all the steps. Everything in social media depends, first and foremost, on creating value for *them* (members of your target audience). Of course, value for them must also create value for you. But if your content is not valuable to your target audience, the audience won't devote time and attention to you. In which case, you will be wasting your time and other resources.

Generically, many strategies can create value for your target audience. These include

- ❑ Educating audience members about issues that they would benefit from understanding (and about which you're an expert).
- ❑ Alerting them to new developments (again, ones that are relevant to them and about which you're an expert).
- ❑ Entertaining them. Who doesn't love a product demonstration or customer testimonial that is humorous or fun?
- ❑ Inspiring them. Do something community-oriented. Everyone loves to help save the world.
- ❑ Saving them money (with coupons, sales, and special offers).
- ❑ Keeping them posted on new product developments.
- ❑ Helping them achieve their goals.

For example, here are value propositions of companies profiled in earlier chapters:

- ❑ Blendtec's YouTube videos illustrated product benefits with humor (entertainment).
- ❑ Hertz tweeted dissatisfied Avis customers and offered those customers discounts and promotions.

❏ Starbucks provided an idea exchange that allowed customers' voices to be heard, resulting in better products and services.

❏ Tween Brands provided stories about raising girls' self-esteem, which helped moms raise their children, and offered 40%-off coupons.

❏ A chiropractor used Twitter Search to engage people with back pain, providing advice to solve a problem.

Pull your team together and brainstorm possibilities. What could you do that is truly valuable to your target audience? Be brutally honest because the success or failure of your every social initiative hangs in the balance.

Step 6: Commit to Specific Tools and Budget

In this step, pick the optimal tool(s) to deliver the intended value to the selected target audience. Keep in mind that the demographics of that audience may affect the choice of tools.

For example, an under-30 group will be excited about a full-scale social networking tool like Facebook or Ning. A 55+ audience, born after the WWII baby boom, will likely be more comfortable with a relatively low-tech blog. A highly mobile group equipped with a variety of mobile phone models may prefer Yammer. Match the tool to the task and the team.

As you consider which tools make sense for your business, tap into the power of Alexa (www.Alexa.com). Alexa offers a handy way to see if the demographics associated with a given service are those of your target audience. Although Alexa is free, you (or your marketing person) will have to install the Alexa toolbar into your browser to unlock Alexa's capability.

With the toolbar installed, go to the Alexa home page and enter the name of any service. Click on the Site Info tab. From there, click on the Audience tab, and you'll get a report. For example, here is the report I received about Pinterest.com.

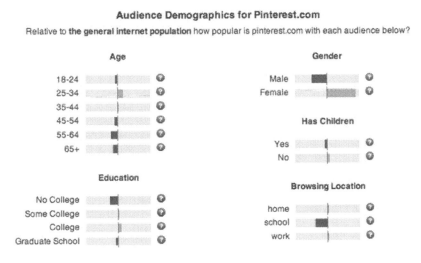

Audience Demographics for Pinterest.com

Relative to **the general internet population** how popular is pinterest.com with each audience below?

This report tells us that Pinterest is used disproportionately by women ages 25–34 who are generally well educated but not currently at school. If this group is part of your target audience (women drive the purchase decisions on homes, cars, dental plans, etc.), you'd better be thinking about Pinterest.

Once you've selected a tool that matches the demographics of your target audience, you will be able to estimate the time your social media initiative will require to implement (including the costs of steps 8–10). This in turn will allow you to establish a budget. Although the external investment may be low, the time to participate, measure, and enhance will have a significant cost.

Chapters 8–17 of this book profile a wide array of social tools for your consideration. Be sure to use Alexa to make sure that tool you choose applies to the demographics of your target audience.

Step 7: Ensure Accountability

It's easy to get excited about the potential of social media. It's equally easy to lose momentum as the demands of business intervene. The most challenging steps of adopting a social media initiative are not steps 1–6. The biggest challenge is achieving the behavioral and/or cultural changes within your organization – the changes that will enable your organization to make effective use of social tools.

As such, identifying a specific owner to drive each initiative is important. The owner, which could be a leader or a team, must be held accountable for implementation and operation of the initiative.

However, the initiative owner is unlikely to be the sole (or even primary) source of compelling content. This is especially true if the owner is in your Marketing Department. Content is most likely also in the heads of multiple "domain experts" throughout your organization. Such players might include product managers, salespeople, engineers (or other technical contributors), Customer Support Team members, and even customers and external partners.

Engage these experts to support your social media initiative owner. As you recruit more participants, distribute the load so the effort required from each contributor is manageable.

If you sell B2C, perhaps content ideas and sources are obvious. If you sell B2B, your most successful customers might be content providers; they could provide case studies and testimonials. The questions most commonly asked of your Customer Support Team may be sources of content. Similarly, key trends in your industry, new technologies (even if not yours), and problems encountered by your competitors (not that you'll call them by name) may also provide ideas for content. With a little brainstorming and creativity, you're likely to discover that your content ideas are virtually limitless.

Not every initiative will succeed. If your best plans don't deliver desired results, fail fast. Just don't fail because of a lack of accountability, compelling content, or effective execution.

Step 8: Define Engagement Metrics

Like a conversation, social media has a certain rhythm. If you are not posting regularly, you're missing an opportunity to be consistently top of mind with your audience; you're missing the chance to become a habit. However, if you're posting too often, you may become overwhelming to your audience. The audience will cut you off.

Social media is a balancing act. Although ample relevant content will improve the position of your content in search results, in many cases your larger opportunity is in building the relationship with your target audience. Don't overwhelm the audience in the quest for search optimization. That's almost always a secondary objective.

As in a conversation, when your audience chooses to engage in dialogue with you through social media, you must respond in a timely way. What constitutes a timely response varies by medium: a minute in text or chat, perhaps an hour (at most) on Facebook, up to one day in a blog. If you exceed the norms of the medium – that is, if you respond too slowly – you'll likely lose the rhythm of the dialogue and lose your audience.

Set explicit participation metrics about how often you'll produce content and how long you'll take to respond to participants. Then design processes and provide resources accordingly.

Step 9: Create Content

As I mentioned earlier, creating compelling content is often easy on day 1, but it becomes increasingly challenging over time. Although your Marketing Department (or marketing person) may be tasked with executing your organization's social media strategy, marketing is not typically the source of the most and best content. The best content is in the heads of your customers and partners, your salespeople, your Customer Support Team, your product people, and your Management Team.

Although the Marketing Department or marketing person may lead your social initiative, everyone should understand the importance of contributing content. If you plan to post weekly to your blog and can identify 13 content contributors inside (and outside) the organization, each of these contributors becomes responsible for just one contribution in a given calendar quarter. That's manageable.

Start by creating a quarterly publication calendar that lists the date of each intended social media post. Place an owner's name next to each date, and ask that person to identify a topic. The marketing contact can then interview each contributor before the due date and draft the piece for review. Even if contributors draft the content themselves, the marketing contact should conduct the final review and be responsible for posting the content on schedule, ensuring a consistent voice.

Blog Publication Calendar

Target Date	Format	Content Contributor	Topic
July 1	Blog post (300–500 words)		
July 15			
July 29			
Aug. 12			

Step 10: Develop a Promotion Plan

No matter how compelling your social media initiatives, they'll be of little value to you if your target audience is unaware of them. Every social media initiative benefits from an explicit promotion plan.

Where are your audience members and how can you reach them? In many cases, they're already engaged online and you can simply go to them. In many cases this is the fastest way to build an audience. However, you must be careful to co-exist with – indeed, add value to – the community as you engage. Members of the community participate for their own purposes, not yours.

Three rich sources of existing audiences include

1. Blogs
    There are more than 200 million blogs, and the number is growing. A specialized search engine such as Technorati (www.Technorati.com) is built for finding blogs by topic. Most important, it provides an authority score for each blog, a measure of audience engagement as defined by readership, commenting, and citing. Authority is ranked on a scale of 1–999, with higher being better. Any triple-

digit blog ranking indicates that the blog has found an audience.

2. LinkedIn groups
    There's a LinkedIn group for almost everything related to business. If by chance there's not a group for your industry or application, you have a golden opportunity to start one. LinkedIn's Groups Directory (www.linkedin.com/directory/groups) allows you to search for existing groups based on a keyword or phrase. Then the directory presents groups ranked by size – largest membership first.

3. Professional and technical forums
    There are countless professional and technical forums in a vast array of industries. Lacking the equivalent of a Technorati or a LinkedIn Groups Directory to rank them, finding relevant forums will take some effort. Start at Google by typing a promising phrase, for example "professional photographers forum." In this case, among the first links provided are www.TheProfessionalPhoto graphyForum.com, www.ThePhotoForum.com, and www.pro4um.com. Having found your audience, comment on a post, ask or answer a question, or share your experience in a helpful way. Engage in your chosen communities while keeping in mind the Pay It Forward Rule. You must contribute content that is valuable to the audience, without selling or self-promoting. In providing content, you may be able to link to your existing blog posts, web pages, etc., when these resources provide relevant detail. Doing so will generate direct traffic from interested parties.

You can also invite a prominent blogger to guest-post on your site or arrange to guest-post on another site. This cross-pollination of audiences can benefit both parties.

There are countless other ways to promote a given social initiative. For example:

❐ Highlight your social media initiative on your home page. Ideally, such a mention should appear "above the fold," perhaps in the upper-right area of the page. Keep in mind that *people don't read anymore,* so use the relevant logo or icon to link to your Facebook page, YouTube channel, etc. Be sure to have resulting clicks open new browser tabs rather than moving people off your site. Ultimately, when visitors leave the social media site, you want them to be back on your home page.

❐ Advertise your social media initiative on your business cards and in your email signatures.

❐ If you do email marketing or any form of periodic newsletter, talk about your social initiative in those vehicles.

❐ Provide a mechanism for your audience to share your social media with their friends. You've no doubt seen these mechanisms countless times, everything from "Forward to a friend" to "Like us on Facebook." When people find something of value, they will want to share it with others. Make it easy by a Forward to a Friend button.

Finally, don't forget the value of personal promotion. Having your team members create awareness of your initiative among the extensive group with whom they have personal contact is a powerful and frequently overlooked opportunity to promote your social content.

Step 11: Measure Results

Social media is measurable. Every business shares at least one goal: to make a profit. So the basic reason to engage in social initiatives – whether internal or external, public or private – is for a positive ROI. I'm not saying there must always be a direct *monetary* return, but any program should be moving you measurably towards your objectives.

Construct your social media initiatives with your intended conversion steps in mind, and assign a value to these conversions. You can then measure the ROI of your external initiatives. Google provides an analytics tool that makes this easy, once you've defined your objectives and conversion steps. Mastering Google Analytics could be the

Scan to learn how
to use
Google Analytics

topic of my next book; in the meantime, you'll find excellent guidance at the Analytics Help Center (https://support.google.com/analytics/?hl=en#topic=3544906).

You can even determine the ROI of your internal initiatives by measuring

❑ Number or quality of employment candidate applications

❑ Employee retention

❑ Reduction in internal email volume (Read about Yammer and Chatter in Chapter 10.)

❑ Improved collaboration and access to information (See TWiki, Chapter 5.)

This is by no means an exhaustive list. Instead, it's a prompt to spur your thinking about the value and measurability of social media and social marketing.

MOVE FORWARD

In business, we rarely undertake a significant initiative without developing a plan. Further, we seldom settle on an approach without first characterizing goals and objectives. Social media should be no different. Follow the 11-step approach laid out in this chapter and document it in writing. Although such documentation should be no longer than a few pages, it will provide a clear road map for achieving success.

Many social media initiatives succeed, but many more fail. Even if they don't fail outright, social initiatives can fail to achieve their full potential. The ideas, examples, principles, and processes you've covered in these first seven chapters have equipped you with knowledge to help you succeed.

Chapters 8–17 of this book cover a specific social tool and associated examples. Instead of reading the remaining chapters chronologically, jump directly to those of greatest relevance to your business.

That said, don't miss Chapter 9, about LinkedIn. Not only is LinkedIn the professionals' social media network, it's almost universally important for all business executives and the only tool covered in this book that is likely to remain significant 10–20 years from now.

Counterpoint

Some people argue that we shouldn't try to quantify the value of our social media initiatives. They argue that you don't calculate the ROI of other discrete business tools, such as cell phones, copiers, employee training, and company meetings. Further, any tool's benefits are tightly intertwined with countless business processes and, therefore, hopelessly complex to assess.

According to this argument, you are able to see that certain tools bring efficiencies and benefits that outweigh their costs. When this is true for a given social media tool (and sometimes it is), have at it – no need to measure.

Further, measurement carries its own costs, which reduces the ROI of a given initiative.

Although these points have merit, it is still good business practice to measure the ROI of any social media initiative. Just because something is challenging is no reason to avoid it. I see too many organizations unsure of their social media ROI and, as a result, failing to invest sufficient resources.

I encourage you to make the effort to understand your potential and actual returns. This will require understanding the conversions that lead your prospects to become customers and making requisite estimates and prudent assumptions about the costs, benefits, and values of associated tools and transitions.

With a calculation of actual value, you'll have a basis for deciding which initiatives merit increased or decreased investment going forward.

Chapter 7 Summary

If you think of your digital presence (aka website and social initiatives) as an online version of a product brochure, you are missing an incredible opportunity. Your digital presence should be a conversion engine optimized to convert visitors into customers. Keep this principle at the forefront when you follow the 11 steps to developing a successful social marketing plan.

Step 1   Define Objective(s) and Conversion Steps

Step 2   Analyze the Competition

Step 3   Identify and Segment the Target Audience(s)

Step 4   Select Keywords

Step 5   Create a Compelling Value Proposition (for the Target Audience)

Step 6   Commit to Specific Tools and Budget

Step 7   Ensure Accountability

Step 8   Define Engagement Metrics

Step 9   Create Content

Step 10   Develop a Promotion Plan

Step 11   Measure Results

SECTION 2

SPECIFIC SOCIAL MEDIA TOOLS

CHAPTER 8

GOOGLE ALERTS AND TWITTER SEARCH: PREPARE TO BE AMAZED

People typically think of social media as a talking tool. Indeed, the word *media* implies creating *content.* However, our social media activity doesn't have to relate to *our* content only. What about *their* content – our customers' and prospects', our employees' and partners'? In business, by using social media we can listen to and learn from what others are saying.

USE GOOGLE ALERTS TO LISTEN

My favorite listening tool is Google Alerts (www.Google.com/alerts). I first touched on this service in Chapter 4. Google's mission is "to organize the world's information and make it universally accessible and useful." Most of us are well practiced at searching Google for what we need. We might say that Google search allows us to find content that is popular.

The Google Alerts service allows you to receive automatic notifications whenever Google finds, on the Web, words and phrases that you specify, as those words and phrases occur in fresh content. Such information may be obscure – content that you'd never find in a Google search. Nonetheless, the content that Google Alerts notifies you about may well be timely and relevant – content that you can use to adapt to a changing marketplace faster than your competition does.

Google Alerts service provides an information advantage in a rapidly changing world. You can use Google Alerts to monitor any kind of information of potential value to your organization, including

- ❑ Your name and your company name (for reputation monitoring)
- ❑ Your product names (for reputation monitoring and detecting potential intellectual property infringement)
- ❑ Your employees' names (for your HR Department to detect potential issues)
- ❑ Customers' names (to keep the Sales Team abreast of developments regarding customers)
- ❑ "Magic" terms – such as *request for proposal,* or RFP – that will help you learn about sales opportunities
- ❑ Prospects' names (for marketing)
- ❑ Competitors' names (for competitive advantage)
- ❑ Partners' and suppliers' names (for building relationships and detecting potential problems)
- ❑ Industry terms or phrases (for accelerating learning)

What part of your company wouldn't benefit from Google Alerts? The service can be helpful in every department.

Do you remember Glassdoor (www.Glassdoor.com) the company-review site mentioned in Chapter 2? If you set a Google Alert on your business name, anytime someone writes about your company on Glassdoor – or anywhere else – Google will notify you.

How might you use this information? Well, among other things, Glassdoor provides an Add Employer Response button. If somebody writes something untrue about your organization, you can set the record straight.

In addition, I use Google Alerts to monitor my own name, Dave Nelsen. Now, you're probably thinking that even with the unconventional spelling there are a lot of Dave Nelsens in the world. You're right, I don't care about the rest of them.

Google provides what might be called a simple mini-programming language to properly focus your alerts. You can find all the details by clicking on the Help link on the main Google Alerts page.

I focus my alerts by using this formula:

"Dave Nelsen" +"Dialog Consulting"

In other words, I type my name, a plus sign, and my company name. I enclose the two word phrases in quotation marks, to define the two word pairs as exact phrases that Google Alerts will search for.

That formula tells Google to notify me only when it sees both phrases on a given site, which eliminates most of the other Dave Nelsens.

Since this single Google Alert won't pick up every mention of me – for example, when I'm mentioned but not linked to my company – I also monitor

"Dave Nelsen" +CEO

That worked well until a company called Giftango promoted some yahoo named Dave Nelsen to be its CEO. So I edited my alert to be

"Dave Nelsen" +CEO -Giftango

That eliminated all of the information about the other guy!

The information I receive with the focused Google Alerts allows me to keep track and respond to what's being said about me.

Imagine the value of getting alerts about your key competitors! For example, imagine you work for a ceiling tile company, Chicago-based CMC Corporation. CMC competes against Armstrong World Industries, which people usually call Armstrong.

If you set an alert on Armstrong, however, you're going to learn a lot about a guy named Lance. So you set your alert as follows:

Armstrong -Lance

Since Lance is dominant in the world of biking and is frequently referred to by just his last name, a better alert might be

Armstrong -Lance -biking

You can have as many excluded terms as you want.

When Neil Armstrong died and was all over the news, you might have edited the alert (no offense):

Armstrong -Lance -biking -Neil

You can further narrow your alert by using AND and OR (all caps) as Boolean operators. (Note: AND and the plus sign are equivalent; recall that the quotation marks designate an exact phrase rather than either of the words.)

Armstrong -Lance -biking -Neil AND "ceiling tile"
OR flooring

You can even focus on Internet subdomains (e.g., the government world) or individual sites (e.g., the website of *The New York Times*) as shown below, respectively:

Armstrong -Lance -biking -Neil AND "ceiling tile"
site:.gov

Armstrong -Lance -biking -Neil AND "ceiling tile"
site:nytimes.com

Google Alerts helps you monitor a tremendous swath of the World Wide Web – including Glassdoor and virtually every other website, 200 million+ blogs, press releases, business pages on Facebook, and lots more – but not Twitter.

TWITTER SEARCH

On Twitter, people speak their minds, in up to 140 characters, roughly 500 million times per day, mostly (80%+) using their mobile devices. Monitoring Twitter is almost like having ESP

– extrasensory perception. When I was a kid, ESP was the one superpower I coveted. I wanted to know exactly what people were thinking. Finally, as I was approaching 50 years old (a few years ago), with Twitter Search I acquired an ability that almost perfectly approximates ESP.

It all starts at https://twitter.com/search-home.

Recall that the location of every mobile phone – as well as every fixed computer – is recorded every 10 seconds. This is true whether a device has GPS capability or not.

Side note: Next time you commit a major felony, leave your phone with your alibi.

Twitter Search combines what people are tweeting with their location data. Think creatively about how your business could use this. For example, let's say you run an auto dealership in Mars (Mars, Pa., that is – my current location). Let's find out who wants a new car *in our neighborhood* right now!

In the Twitter Search box, we type: "new car" (in quotation marks, to search for the entire phrase). And since we serve a limited geographic area, we'll add a zip code reference: "near:16046" (without quotation marks). To be more specific, we'll also specify "within:25 miles" (without quotation marks) because people will drive only so far for a good deal. The actual search query looks like this:

"new car" near:16046 within:25mi

In just 1.93 seconds, we discover the tweets of four local folks with new cars on their minds:

1. "MY **NEW CAR** IS GONNA BE A 2015 CAR"

2. "Scramble and find a **new car** – my inspection is up and costs way too much to fix. 188k miles!"

3. "I wanna **New Car**!!!"

4. "It's time for a **new car**!"

In each case, we could begin a conversation by offering something of value to the tweeter – per the Pay It Forward Rule – perhaps a secret discount code or helpful advice such as: "I'm a car dealer. Inside info: You always get a better deal when you … " (Not being a car dealer myself, I'd love to see the next 72 characters of this advice.)

One other thing: Once you've created a search query that works, you can set it for continuous operation. You'll receive automatic notifications as new matches occur in real time. How cool is that?

To receive automatic notifications, you'll need a fabulous Twitter tool called TweetDeck (https://tweetdeck.twitter.com/). This is what an alert looks like when configured to show mentions of back pain and new car in my geography:

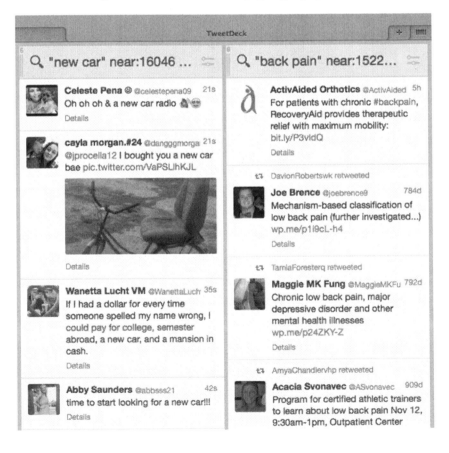

Using ESP (aka Twitter Search) for your business, in your geography, and then engaging within the norms of social media, you can find and win new customers.

Tune in to anything that's important to you, including people with positive or negative attitudes (customer service, anyone?), people posing questions, and people referring to your business (or your competitors). The possibilities are limited only by your creativity.

The entire range of Twitter Search operators is shown below.

Operator	Finds tweets...
twitter search	containing both "twitter" and "search". This is the default operator.
"happy hour"	containing the exact phrase "happy hour".
love OR hate	containing either "love" or "hate" (or both).
beer -root	containing "beer" but not "root".
#haiku	containing the hashtag "haiku".
from:alexiskold	sent from person "alexiskold".
to:techcrunch	sent to person "techcrunch".
@mashable	referencing person "mashable".
"happy hour" near:"san francisco"	containing the exact phrase "happy hour" and sent near "san francisco".
near:NYC within:15mi	sent within 15 miles of "NYC".
superhero since:2010-12-27	containing "superhero" and sent since date "2010-12-27" (year-month-day).
ftw until:2010-12-27	containing "ftw" and sent up to date "2010-12-27".
movie -scary :)	containing "movie", but not "scary", and with a positive attitude.
flight :(	containing "flight" and with a negative attitude.
traffic ?	containing "traffic" and asking a question.
hilarious filter:links	containing "hilarious" and linking to URLs.
news source:twitterfeed	containing "news" and entered via TwitterFeed

Keep Information Organized with Email Rules

One potential problem with Google Alerts is that the service can generate substantial additional email. Perhaps you'll feel more popular as your Inbox fills up ever faster, but most of us are not looking for that.

You could send your alerts to a separate email account, but you'd probably forget to monitor it.

Instead, create an email rule. Yes, this is the one time that both Steve Jobs and Bill Gates made a task easy on us. In both Outlook and Apple Mail, the capability goes by the same name, rules. In Gmail, the function is called filters. Most other email systems have a similar feature.

By whatever name, a rule processes incoming email based on a set of conditions. The syntax of the condition statement varies, but the logic is essentially as follows.

If message is from googlealerts-noreply@google.com, move message to target folder.

When you're busy, you can ignore your alerts. But when you have time for *information advantage*, and who doesn't, you can blast through the alerts quickly, focusing on those that are most meaningful to your business.

After you implement a rule for Google Alerts, you'll want to create rules for many other things:

If message is from any of these current clients or hot prospects, then move message to "Priority" folder.

Priority messages are always the first that I review after accessing my Inbox. Consider this rule:

If message is from any of these senders, then move message to Trash.

You've got to love that.

The logic that follows would be useful as a rule:

If message is from FollowUpThen.com, then move message to FollowUp folder.

FollowUpThen (www.FollowUpThen.com/) is a fabulous free email reminder service. Check it out.

Rules are invaluable. I've recently found a service that discovers your email patterns and implements rules for you automatically. It's not free, but the aptly named SaneBox (www.SaneBox.com) is likely worth every penny.

CHAPTER 8 SUMMARY

- ❐ Social media can be used not just to dialogue, but to listen and learn.

- ❐ Use Google Alerts to listen for information of value to your organization, including talk about your company name, employees' names, customers' and prospects' names, competitors, and much more.

- ❐ Narrow your alerts by using the operators AND, OR, +, -, site:, etc. Using the operators will help ensure that the information you receive is relevant and valuable to you.

- ❐ Use Twitter Search to listen for information of value to your organization in the geographies you serve.

- ❐ Use Twitter's TweetDeck tool to be updated automatically as search matches occur.

- ❐ Develop an engagement strategy to capitalize on the new business opportunities that you discover using both Google Alerts and Twitter Search.

CHAPTER 9

LinkedIn:
Join the Professionals'
Social Network

Maybe you've played or heard of the trivia game Six Degrees of Kevin Bacon. The idea is that actor Bacon's work is so prolific and diverse that any Hollywood actor can be linked to any other in a handful of steps, based on their associations with Bacon. The name of the game derives from the idea of six degrees of separation, the theory that everyone is six or fewer relationships away from any other person in the world. According to the theory, a chain of "a friend introducing a friend" can connect any two people in six steps or fewer.

LinkedIn (www.linkedin.com), the social media tool popular with professionals, assumes a person needs just three degrees of connection. My own experience shows the most valuable part of LinkedIn actually consists of the two-degree connections.

LinkedIn works like this: You know Jim; Jim knows Sue. Therefore, you are two degrees away from Sue. More important, Jim knows both of you and can act as a connector. If Sue looks like a promising client or partner, you ask Jim to introduce the two of you, ideally IRL (in real life) over coffee or lunch. Consider the difference between this introduction versus making a cold call to Sue.

The math on two-degree connections is impressive. Recently, I had just over 800 direct LinkedIn connections. Factoring in all of those associates' connections (i.e., by using second-degree connections), I can reach the almost 400,000 business professionals who they know. That's approximately 500 times more people than I know directly. Even without understanding anything else about LinkedIn, you can appreciate its exponential power for relationship mapping.

An Important Digression: Think Quality Connections, Not Quantity

Before going further, there is one extremely important concept to keep in mind when using LinkedIn. You should request and accept direct connections with known and trusted business associates only. When it comes to connections, LinkedIn is about quality, not quantity.

Your network will degrade to useless (or worse) the more often you connect with people you don't know or don't respect. In building connections, ask yourself these three questions:

1. Do I know this person professionally?
2. Do I respect this person professionally? (As Dr. Evil says in the Austin Powers movies, "Why must I be surrounded by idiots?")
3. Would I be happy to help this person with something if he or she asked me?

When the answer to all three questions is yes, the connection request is coming from someone you can assist in making professional connections to help sell products or services, find great partners, and recruit outstanding employees. Most important, that person can do the same for you.

If you've made the mistake of accepting every connection request that came your way, you're what I call a promiscuous connector. See my advice on unlinking; it's at the end of this chapter.

Indeed, feel free to "Ignore" connection requests from people who don't meet your criteria. With LinkedIn, a requester will not know you ignored his or her request. There's no explicit notification (or slap in the face) to tell this person he or she has been ignored.

Of course, if someone is overtly spamming you with requests, click on the Report Spam button instead. If other people do the same, LinkedIn will punish the perpetrator by limiting his or her functionality.

Although choosing connections you trust creates a powerful network, you still might not want your connections to see all your other connections, which happens by default with LinkedIn. If your connections represent your existing customers, your hot prospects, and your best employees and partners, others could use that information to your disadvantage. To prevent this, I recommend turning off connection visibility.

To do so, move your cursor so it hovers over your name in the upper-right screen area and select Settings. You'll land on a screen that includes a variety of options under Profile. Click on "Select who can see your connections" and set it to "Only you." As LinkedIn will tell you, people will still be able to see shared connections, a highly valuable aspect of LinkedIn, but this represents just a small fraction (perhaps less than 1%) of your network relative to any given searcher.

GET STARTED WITH LINKEDIN

If you're not yet a member of LinkedIn, get started by signing up. Go to www.linkedin.com and you'll see a simple sign-up form. Provide your name, email address (aka username), and specify a password. You'll be on your way.

To join LinkedIn, sign up below...it's free!

First Name:

Last Name:

Email:

New Password:

6 or more characters

Join LinkedIn *

Already on LinkedIn? Sign in

After clicking on Join LinkedIn, LinkedIn will ask you for some basic employment information to start building your network. It typically takes just a few minutes to provide this data.

Next you'll be asked to confirm your email address and then to sign in again.

Finally, you'll reach a screen that will allow you to see who you already know on LinkedIn. Remembering the three rules above, please *do not* import your entire contact list from Outlook (etc.) and invite each contact to connect. In truth, you probably don't really know one-quarter of your contacts, let alone want to spend your time helping them with anything. Nor would they help you.

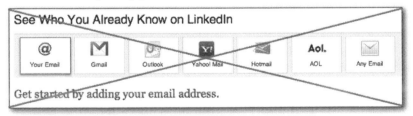

Instead, take time to review your list of connection candidates carefully and select only those people with whom you truly want to connect. Alternatively, notice the options to "Invite by individual email" or "Upload [selected] contacts file." This last option may be the best way to jumpstart your network with high-quality connections.

As you use LinkedIn, you'll notice that the system will occasionally suggest that you connect with people you may know. In my experience, the software is surprisingly prescient, so it's worth paying attention to its suggestions. When you recognize someone who would be an ideal connection, reach out to that person with a customized message (as opposed to the generic, system-generated "I'd like to add you to my professional network on LinkedIn"), explaining why you'd like to (re)connect.

Over time, be sure to complete the rest of your profile. (LinkedIn will remind you periodically.) Why? According to the company, "Users with complete profiles are 40 times more likely to receive opportunities (including job offers) through LinkedIn."

UNLEASH THE POWER OF YOUR LINKEDIN NETWORK
Use your LinkedIn network in these powerful ways:

1. Gather information about competitors and develop insights about customers and prospects.
2. Network and prospect for sales.
3. Participate in Industry Groups and Discussions.
4. Recruit and check references. (Using LinkedIn to do this is also a great way to find your next job, but that's a topic for a different book.)
5. Build your brand by using a Company Page.

1. Gather Information About Competitors and Develop Insights About Customers and Prospects

In my entire professional career, I've never found anything more valuable than talking to my competitors' former employees. I'm not talking about accessing confidential information or committing corporate espionage. For example, in Chapter 4, I told the story about starting

TalkShoe, and how "Barry," a former employee of a competitor, gave me a key insight that was at the core of my company's ultimate success.

Would it help your company to get a few new insights about your toughest competitors? About a new prospect, a potential partner, or a job candidate? What if you could connect with someone who has "inside insights" about a competitor (without violating any confidentiality rules)?

Regarding *former* employees of any company, be it a competitor, a prospective customer, or a possible partner:

- ❑ There are many of these people. Most companies have twice as many former employees listed as current employees listed.
- ❑ These people know a lot of stuff. Often they've been selling against you. They may know exactly what your weaknesses are and how you can improve.
- ❑ They'll tell you *anything.* There's little, if any, loyalty to former employers these days. And since your company is in their industry, you're a potential future employer. They want to impress you. Further, people love to talk about what they know, to show how smart they are or to be helpful. You need make no promises or representations; just ask your questions and let them talk.

What would you like to know about a key customer, competitor, or prospect? There is nothing to limit you here but your own imagination. On LinkedIn, use an Advanced People Search to find a former insider who is willing to share his or her priceless insights and guidance. You'll use this same feature to network and prospect for sales. I'll explain exactly how this works in the next section.

2. Network and Prospect for Sales

You know that a warm introduction beats a cold call. You know also that trust is fundamental to selling. LinkedIn is the ideal vehicle for getting warm introductions through mutually trusted associates. Here's how:

When signed in on the LinkedIn home page, you'll notice the People Search box in the upper right. Immediately to the right of that, see the Advanced button. Click on the button to access Advanced People Search mode.

Notice that you can search (free) for virtually any combination of attributes, including

- First name
- Last name
- Title (current or past)
- Company (current or past)
- Keywords
- Location (within a specified radius of any given zip code)
- School
- Industry
- Relationship (as in degrees of separation – the most valuable attribute)

LinkedIn also has a number of other filters that are restricted to the premium service, which starts at $20/month when billed annually. These include

- Seniority level (which you can typically access with the Title option, which is free)
- Job function
- Years of experience
- Company size
- Fortune ranking (as in Fortune 500)

You might wonder whether you should pay for LinkedIn's premium service. For salespeople, the free attributes of Advanced People Search are usually sufficient for finding the right people to aid sales. On the other hand, if you're using LinkedIn for recruiting potential employees, it may be worth paying for the "Years of experience" filter, among others.

Your ability to find someone in the LinkedIn community (aka 300 million professionals, of whom roughly half are in the United States) is limited only by the search combinations you're willing to try. I strongly encourage you to experiment with this. Prepare to be amazed.

For example, using my own network and searching for CEOs within 50 miles of my current location, I find 5,175 matches.

To narrow from all members meeting a given criteria to just second-degree connections, scan the list of filters down the left side. You'll see that All LinkedIn Members is checked in an initial search. Just below that, select Second Connections instead. A search of my network yields 1,420 CEOs who are second-degree connections – people to whom I can get introduced by a connection who knows both of us. If that doesn't impress you, you must possess a certain sales magic that I've never seen.

Once you've identified a target person, there's a link to shared connections. Click on that link and you'll see a list of names (with pictures) of all the people who are mutual acquaintances or connections. Select the one you know best and call or email that person to ask for an introduction to your target.

If for some reason your first-choice connector can't or won't make an introduction, go back to your list of shared connections and try again. Don't be afraid to be creative – you will be impressed at the caliber of people to whom you can get a warm introduction.

3. Participate in Industry Groups and Discussions

Of all the LinkedIn features, which allow me to do amazing things, I spend more time using the Industry Groups and Discussions feature than any other. By participating in groups with professionals in your own industry (aka birds of a feather), you can get answers to your questions simply by posting them to the group and receiving input from countless other professionals and experts.

As a social media practitioner, I participate in the groups called Social Media Today and Social Media Marketing to interact with more than 100,000 industry professionals. Why learn alone when I can learn from everyone? Remember, *none of us is as smart as all of us.*

It's easy to find groups that are relevant to you. When signed in on your LinkedIn home page, select the Groups option from the main menu. Under the Groups menu, you'll see Groups Directory. Enter a keyword, and you'll see all the groups that relate to the keyword, ranked from largest to smallest. On the off chance that an appropriate group does not already exist, you have an excellent opportunity to position yourself as a thought leader or expert in your industry by clicking on the Create a Group button and taking the lead.

Talk about accelerated learning! Whatever you might want to know, a "mastermind" group (such as the groups on LinkedIn tend to be) will probably provide the answer. You can access the wisdom of crowds – very smart crowds – in exactly your area of need.

Consider joining a second type of group as well: the type of group in which your customers and prospects participate. Again, use the Groups Directory to find them. When participants ask questions in your domain, answer them. It's a chance to create visibility for your company while demonstrating your expertise. Without being a self-promoter, you'll draw people to you.

4. Recruit and Check References

I've hired dozens of high-priced salespeople in my career ($250,000+ in total compensation) and found they have just one thing in common. Whether they're God's gift to sales or the worst thing since the Edsel, they're all masters at selling themselves. If you combine this with the fact that the best people rarely (as in never) have their resumes on Monster.com (they find the next great opportunity from the strength of their current position), your chance of success using traditional hiring methods is about the same as the probability of being abducted by aliens (the UFO kind).

Perhaps that's why a reported "80% of companies are now using LinkedIn as a primary tool to find employees." (Although this statistic is impressive, it's worth bearing in mind that 63.2% of statistics are made up. Still, it's likely to be in the general ballpark.)

LinkedIn has a powerful set of premium features for re-cruiting (see the Jobs option in the main menu). That said, I prefer to use the free, less formal methods. Some tech-niques for locating and vetting potential employees fol-low.

Begin by asking your first-degree (aka direct) connections who they know who might be an excellent candidate for a given position. Ideally, that position is already highlighted in the Careers section of your Company Page (keep read-ing). You'll be pleasantly surprised at the quality of peo-ple who surface based on suggestions from the people you know and respect.

You can make this request in two different ways: From your LinkedIn home page, type the question into your status box (aka "Share an update"). This will post your question as a status update to all of your connections.

Or click on "Connections" (under Contacts in the main menu), select individuals who you'd like to query directly, and then click on "Send message." Include an explanation like this: "It's okay if a suggested person is not necessarily looking for a new position; that's probably a good thing."

Either way, you're likely to receive a number of responses.

Next, for vetting potential hires, LinkedIn is even more helpful. I strongly believe in checking references before hiring someone. But of the literally hundreds of references I've checked (as provided by my candidates), I've never, ever, ever had someone give me a bad reference.

What kind of a sociopath can't gin up three good references? If I give my brother a bottle of Scotch and a few cigars, he'll say anything! Direct references are almost guaranteed to be good and are, therefore, a waste of time. And don't even try calling the prior employer's HR Department. I can already tell you: "The employee left on good terms."

Reference checking is a premium feature that will set you back $20 per month. I bet there's nothing in business that can give you a better ROI.

Here's how it works: Go to LinkedIn and view a person's profile. Immediately next to the blue button that says "Send a message," you'll see a small down-arrow. Click on it and select the option "Find references." This will most likely give you numerous second-degree references who have *not* already been coached to lie through their teeth about your prospective candidate. I call this blind reference checking. One candid blind reference check could save you the huge cost (in time, money, and pain) of a bad hire.

5. **Build Your Brand by Using a Company Page**

    Not so long ago, LinkedIn expanded from being about
    people to also being about companies, with the addition of
    LinkedIn Company Pages. These pages allow you to pro-
    vide updates about your company, post information about
    careers, and share information about your products and
    services. People can follow your company to learn more
    about you. Prospects can (and often will) visit your Com-
    pany Page before deciding to do business with you or
    with a competitor. Make sure that your page is better than
    your competitor's.

    The best way to get started on a Company Page is by re-
    viewing some of the best models out there. Here are the
    URLs of a few that I admire, from among those recog-
    nized by LinkedIn as the best of the best:

    ❐ http://lnkd.in/adobe
    ❐ http://lnkd.in/cnbc
    ❐ http://lnkd.in/hubspot (FYI: HubSpot is a great tool
        for managing your social initiatives.)
    ❐ http://lnkd.in/magnapowertrain (This page is an out-
        standing B2B example.)
    ❐ http://lnkd.in/TataConsultancy (This page provides
        an excellent model for featuring professional ser-
        vices.)

    Notice that each has a compelling company description
    and updates that both inform and invite conversation.
    There's nothing static on a good Company Page. Once
    again, social media is all about conversation.

    To get started creating your own Company Page, click on
    Companies in the main menu and click on Add a Company
    link, in the upper-right screen area. Follow the model you
    like best, and keep the page active rather than static.

LEARN ABOUT UNLINKING

If along the way you've made the mistake of linking to a number of people who are not your trusted, known associates, unlinking is an important task. Instructions follow.

1. Click on "Contacts," in the main menu on the LinkedIn home page.
2. Click on "Remove Connections," in the upper-right corner of the Connections view.
3. Select the people you'd like to remove from your Connections list by checking the box next to their names.
4. Click on the "Remove Connections" button.

People will not be notified that they have been removed from your connections list. Instead, they will be added to your list of imported contacts, just in case you want to re-invite them to connect later. And happily, only the member who breaks the connection can reinitiate that connection.

Where Is Everybody?

While LinkedIn now has over 200 million members (aka accounts), in any given month only about one-third of those members log onto the site even once. That means that two-thirds of members are not really using the service. That's okay. For this reason, LinkedIn is a relatively poor tool for actually connecting, but it's a great tool for discovering relationships (who knows whom). There are many ways to connect in the real world.

While I'm not against sending InMail (a premium feature) or clicking on Get Introduced, these techniques are more likely than not to fail. Don't stop there.

Instead, email or pick up the phone, contacting the intermediary who can connect you to the person you're trying to reach. Remember, this person is a known professional connection who you would be glad to help (as outlined early in this chapter). As such, he or she is likely to be willing to help you.

Always ask your intermediary how well he or she knows the person you're trying to reach. If your intermediary is a promiscuous connector and doesn't actually know the person, consider using another connector. Consider unlinking from the person who's just failed you.

Chapter 9 Summary

☐ LinkedIn, the social network popular with professionals, is based on the concept of degrees of separation. LinkedIn assumes that you are just three relationships away from a valuable introduction you need to move forward. My experience shows that even a second-degree relationship can yield impressive results.

☐ In choosing connections, limit yourself to people you know and trust. A powerful network consists of high-quality connections, not a high quantity of them.

☐ A good connection is one about whom you can answer yes to *all* of the following questions:

1. Do I know this person professionally?
2. Do I respect this person professionally?
3. Would I be happy to help this person if he or she asked me?

☐ Unleash the power of connections by using LinkedIn in the following ways:

1. Gather information about competitors and develop insights about customers and prospects.
2. Network and prospect for sales.
3. Participate in Industry groups and discussions.
4. Recruit and check references.
5. Build your brand by using a Company Page.

CHAPTER 10

IMPROVE EMPLOYEE COMMUNICATION: YAMMER AND CHATTER

I'm frequently asked, "Dave, what's the next big thing?" My typical answer is, "If I knew that, I wouldn't be standing here talking to you."

That said, a few key trends are worth noting: The mobile revolution, location-based services, augmented reality,[5] and group texting.

In early 2014, Facebook paid $19 billion for a group texting app called WhatsApp. If group texting is *that* important, perhaps your business and mine can use it to enhance communication. Indeed. Two corporate group texting services are Yammer (www.Yammer.com), which is now owned by Microsoft, and Chatter (www.salesforce.com/chatter/overview/), part of Salesforce.

Recall that Osama Bin Laden story in Chapter 2? That same process of unlocking and integrating collective knowledge

---

[5] Most people are already familiar with augmented reality, or AR, but may not know the term. If you've ever watched football on television, you know that yellow stripe that marks the first-down yard line. It's nowhere to be found in an actual stadium. It's a computer-generated graphics overlay on the live video stream. With smart devices now equipped with workstation-class processors, you're about to see a lot more AR, in this case for personal use. AR is a likely candidate to drive QR codes to extinction because, with sufficient processing power, recognizing an image is as easy as reading a black-and-white code.

can happen among your employees, if they're using Yammer or Chatter.

In a November 2013 study, McKinsey & Company, a global consulting company, estimated that "about two-thirds of social's estimated economic value [will stem] from improved collaboration and communication within enterprises."

Until now, you were probably thinking of social media as a tool for marketing and external communication.

If you've never used group texting, it's the same thing as regular texting but, instead of being one-to-one, it's one-to-many or many-to-many. Yammer and Chatter add numerous features: Examples include tagging; searching; following; and, perhaps most important, unfollowing. All these features are available to your company in a private group-texting cloud.

Since the basic versions of Yammer and Chatter are free, why not try an experiment in your organization rather than reading more service descriptions? Inevitably, the hard part is not figuring out what these tools can do or even understanding how to use them. The challenge is in changing employee behavior and corporate culture.

Find a small team of volunteers (not draftees) to try Yammer or Chatter. Pick one narrow application to see how it affects collaboration.

Examples of possible applications include

- ❏ Quickly getting expert answers to field personnel
- ❏ Solving customers' problems
- ❏ Sharing knowledge about competitors' tactics
- ❏ Providing company news (customer wins, new products, etc.)

Remember to stay firmly focused on the Pay It Forward Rule: The initiative *must be valuable to your target audience* – in this case your employees, not your customers and prospects.

Executive participation (aka yours) is likely to bring more focus and momentum to your trial. Your goal is to discover where you can create new efficiencies (likely by reducing email) or performance improvements (faster access to more accurate information) for your team.

If you find no value, fail fast and try a different application. However, if like 10s of thousands of other companies, your company realizes new business benefits, then begin a wider rollout. Start by writing a short document that explains how and, more important, when and why to use Yammer or Chatter. Otherwise, employees may be confused about when to use group texting vs. email (vs. phone call vs. face-to-face communication).

An example of use guidelines follows. I crafted these guidelines with a commercial construction services client.

Our Yammer Use Guidelines

In considering Yammer, our objectives are to enhance internal communication effectiveness and efficiency; to provide a single-source platform, for communicating messages consistently to employees, that eliminates duplication; to make organizing, finding, and sharing information easier; to strengthen the bonds of our employee community; to reduce the amount of internal email.

Our closed (employee-only) Yammer community will be a platform for delivering a singular message to our distributed employee base, to help achieve geographic unification, and to provide our team members with real-time information on their terms. It will also allow efficient access to information by the entire team, with individuals deciding which colleagues are most valuable to follow.

We'll identify and activate an initial feature set (biasing towards fewer features in the beginning, to simplify adoption, with additional features activated over time) and solicit input on usage guidelines. We'll have a small set of volunteers pilot the initial implementation before inviting all employees to join. We'll produce a screen capture–

based demo to show how to use the platform and will post (and promote, via regular email blasts) fresh corporate content every week, to model proper usage.

Our goal is to pilot Yammer for three months, at which time we'll conduct a review and assess the best applications and relative value of each. Assuming that we move forward with full-scale rollout (or even selected-target or narrow applications), we will achieve significant adoption and corporate culture change within the first 12 months of adoption. Specific participation measures are to be defined but will involve use compliance, quality of content, ease of access to content, and reduction in email volume.

After full activation, we'll consistently communicate our utilization philosophy, constantly reinforcing both the expectations and the benefits of corporate adoption. We'll do this via email, company newsletters, and group meetings, highlighting success stories as they occur.

And finally, we'll publicize and reinforce Yammer use with the following use statement:

We recognize that *None of us is as smart as all of us*. The purpose of Yammer is to share information that can be of benefit to our colleagues, to help them succeed in their endeavors. We will be respectful of their time and attention, focusing on information that promotes our corporate culture and values and that helps us better serve our customers.

We aim to empower individuals to invest their time more effectively, specifically by stemming the flood of email and providing more efficient mechanisms based on pull, rather than push (i.e., allowing the content consumer to determine what to access and follow).

We use Yammer as a dialogue tool, sharing timely, valuable information about customers and prospects, business issues, competitors, and other business happenings, etc.

We use the following hashtags to help organize information,:

#SalesOpportunity (potential new business)

#CustomerProblem

#CompetitorTactic

#IndustryNews (industry updates)

#CompanyNews

#Win (new customers and projects)

We do NOT post updates about personal activities, vacations, lunch choices, or other trivia.

We collectively encourage and reinforce (through compliments, thanks, and so on) the best uses of Yammer. Conversely, we discourage and provide feedback on inappropriate uses.

We use Yammer as a document management system for sharing those documents, including presentations and memos, that have value for distributed members of our organization in the near term and over time. This includes (among others) HR documents, travel expense forms, etc.

We will NOT post information that is private or of one-to-one value. (Such documents are better shared by email.)

We periodically review Yammer Case Studies (www.yammer.com/customers/), to expand our thinking.

Given that your challenge will be in changing team behavior, consider a fun way to get your employees engaged in
driving that change.

With your Yammer guidelines in hand, give every employee an envelope of 10 fresh $1 bills. Whenever an employ-
ee catches someone misusing Yammer – or more likely, still
using email when Yammer would be the better vehicle – that
person can fine the offender $1. Of course, that person is also
subject to fines. See how long it takes behavior to change
when money and pride are on the line.

The potential Yammer or Chatter benefits outlined at the
end of Chapter 2 are compelling. Consider for a moment the
value to everyone in your organization of a 30% decline in
email! That's worth doing your first small experiment.

Chapter 10 Summary

- ❒ McKinsey & Company, a global consulting firm,
  estimates that "about two-thirds of social's estimated economic value [will stem] from improved
  collaboration and communication within enterprises."

- ❒ Chatter and Yammer are two leading free social
  media tools for enhancing internal communication.

- ❒ Try experimenting with one of these tools, exploring a specific communication- or collaboration-
  enhancement opportunity.

- ❒ Recruit a team of volunteers and at least one company executive.

- ❒ Remember that the initiative *must be valuable to
  your target audience* – in this case, your employees.

- ❒ Review results after three months.

- ❒ If successful, develop written use guidelines and
  begin a wider rollout.

❏ Define a set of useful hashtags (e.g., #CustomerProblem) to help organize and access information.

❏ To drive adoption, publicize successes by using the old tools (email, company meetings, etc.).

❏ Use your corporate culture (and a possible system of fines) to reinforce desired behavior.

CHAPTER 11

FACEBOOK:
IS IT FOR COLLEGE KIDS OR BUSINESS?

Is Facebook, the tool that began with college kids connecting with friends, the ideal forum for your business? It depends.

Facebook has certainly evolved from its roots in the college environment. If you sell B2C, Facebook can be a powerful tool. If you sell B2B, Facebook is less likely to be effective. For B2B companies, Google+ is the better bet. See this chapter's sidebar.

One of the biggest benefits of social media tools is customer dialogue. With more than 1.2 billion members, more than half of whom have been active in the last 30 days, Facebook is a great place to have conversations with consumers. Through conversations, you learn what potential customers want, and they learn what your business offers. The faster your employees learn, the better they can serve your customers. The better prospects and customers know what you offer, the more likely you are to find your sweet spot with them.

To attract target-audience members to your dialogue, remember to follow the three rules of social media. It's not enough to *have* a Facebook page, you have to follow the Cocktail Party Rule, remember PIE, and follow the Pay It Forward Rule.

Facebook's powerful potential regarding B2C users extends beyond dialogue. With its many active users, Facebook can be a venue for free PR. In the beginning, of course, Facebook was just about connecting with "friends." I hope it doesn't hurt your feelings, but businesses don't have friends.

In Facebook lingo, businesses that satisfy or even delight customers, by fulfilling their needs more effectively than competitors, have "fans" who "Like." Any satisfied customer can press a button to Like a business's page on Facebook.

When that fan decides to Like your business, his or her friends see that you have received a peer endorsement, the most valuable form of free PR. According to the Edelman Trust Barometer (http://www.edelman.com/insights/intellectual-property/2014-edelman-trust-barometer), more than 75% of people trust what they hear about your business from their peers but just 17% trust what you say about yourself.

To use Facebook effectively, engage customers and prospects in a dialogue and give them a reason to Like your business.

GET STARTED WITH FACEBOOK

As a quick reminder, before you start with Facebook, as with any social initiative, ensure that you have outstanding products and services that are clearly differentiated from those of your competition. Make sure your offerings are well serviced with solid customer support. Social media is an accelerator; it makes strong companies more successful sooner and weak companies, well, bankrupt. In social media, word spreads quickly either way.

Also before you start, make sure Facebook fits into your social media plan by following the 11-step process detailed in Chapter 7. Even though Facebook is free, engaging in a Facebook campaign is not, at least in terms of time and energy.

Once you decide that investing time in Facebook is a good business decision, go to the Facebook home page. You'll see a button in the lower right that says, "Create a Page for a celebrity, band, or business." Click there.

You'll land on a page that offers six choices:

1. Local Business or Place
2. Company, Organization, or Institution

3. Brand or Product

4. Artist, Band or Public Figure

5. Entertainment

6. Cause or Community

Choose the option that best fits your business. Don't worry if the fit is not exact; you're selecting a template, not a directory listing.

Next you'll see a drop-down list with dozens of subcategories. Again, pick the closest fit.

From there, you'll find it easy to complete your Facebook business page and begin customizing content about your company.

A Facebook business page, when compared to a Facebook nonbusiness page, has many benefits. Foremost among these benefits is that business pages are open to everybody, even Facebook nonmembers. In addition, Google indexes business pages, so everything on your business page helps improve the page's ranking in search results.

For a case study of using Facebook successfully, return to http://www.Facebook.com/Starbucks. Over four years, Starbucks' number of Likes increased from 1,754,451 to more than 36 million. If the size and resources of Starbucks are intimidating to you, don't worry. I'll present a case study of a small business that uses Facebook successfully.

Why do people visiting any Facebook business page click on the Like button? According to one survey, here are the reasons:

To get discounts and promotions	40%
To get freebies (e.g., samples)	36%
To get updates on future products	33%
To get updates on upcoming sales	30%
For fun or entertainment	29%
For access to exclusive content	25%

For education about company topics   13%

To interact (i.e., to provide feedback)   13%

(Some respondents chose multiple reasons, so the numbers total to more than 100%.)

As I write this chapter, a lot is happening on the Starbucks page. Among other things, the company is sharing descriptions and photos of the Starbucks CEO's trip to Rwanda and dialoguing with customers about Starbucks products. A recent post reads, "Discover the Treat Receipt, and bring in your receipt from this morning for a Grande $2 cold drink."

In this post, Starbucks is playing to the most common reason that people click on Like – to get discounts and promotions. In fact, one secret to attracting 36 million Starbucks fans is Free Pastry Day. It works like this.

Tuesday is the slowest weekday at Starbucks. On the projected slowest Tuesday each month (presumably, Starbucks has excellent historical data and predictive powers), Starbucks declares that it is Free Pastry Day. This special day is not advertised on the website or in stores. Free Pastry Day is posted exclusively on Facebook and Twitter so that the occasion drives social chatter.

When you, as a fan of Starbucks on Facebook, see the announcement, you don't need to print a coupon. Instead, just hustle down to your local store before 10:30 a.m., display the announcement on your mobile device, order any drink, and get any pastry free.

When I do this, the person behind me in line invariably asks how I did that. I mention Liking Starbucks on Facebook, and the person hustles back to his or her computer or (more likely) pulls out a smartphone, fires up the Facebook app, and clicks on Like. Then, no doubt, my fellow customer waits for the next Free Pastry Day to be announced.

Would you like to guess which day each month is the busiest day at Starbucks?

Before you conclude that this Facebook thing is only for the big guys, notice that a search for "Facebook dentist" returns more than 500 matches. Hey, if a dentist can get people to click on Like, how hard could it be? Remember once again that there are more than 1.2 billion members of Facebook and that more than half have been active there during the past 30 days.

Still, I admit that, in a way, the Starbucks example is misleading. In social networking, *quality actually trumps quantity.* Social media is about creating a real conversation with those people who are most interested in what you offer and about accelerating your learning and theirs. It's easier to sell to and serve someone who is fully engaged in such a conversation because you understand that person's needs and expectations at a level that was nearly impossible to achieve in the past.

Social media realities can actually favor smaller companies over larger ones. I've seen many instances of customers delighting in connecting with small or local businesses (and businesspeople) that they love. Because of the manageable scale, it's easier for small businesses to use Facebook to engage in authentic conversations with their fans than for large businesses to do so.

One outstanding example of a small business that uses Facebook very effectively is Hicks Nurseries, the oldest garden center on Long Island. Hicks is a family business that's been around for more than 160 years. In September 2011, I was lucky enough to meet Stephen Hicks, president and sixth generation of the Hicks family to be involved in the nursery.

Hicks Nurseries is surviving and thriving in a world of "big box" competitors. Hicks does many things well throughout its operation, not the least of which is engaging customers at www.facebook.com/HicksNurseries.

As a small business operating from a single location, Hicks has attracted almost 10,000 Likes. That's impressive, but the value of a Like is limited if customers are not also engaged.

Facebook provides two measures, or metrics, of audience engagement. The definitions are likely to evolve, but as I write here they are.

1. The metric "were here" represents how many Facebook check-ins and mobile device location shares a company has attracted recently. The interval is unspecified. (By the way, this measure is available only when a company includes its address(es) on its Facebook business page. Be sure to do so: "were here" is a modern proxy for measures of foot traffic.)

2. The metric "Facebook people who are talking about this," represents unique visitors during the previous seven days who do any of the following:

    • Post on your page

    • Like your page or Like a given post

    • Comment on or share a post

    • Mention your page in a post

    • Answer a question (Note to self: Ask more questions.)

    • Write a recommendation (Note to self: Ask for more customer recommendations.)

    • Claim an offer

    • Engage in a half dozen other possible interactions

The Hicks model is impressive because of the level of *engagement* of the business's Facebook audience. According to Facebook, 93.4% of Hicks' Likers *"were here"* recently, and fully 5% of Hicks Likers were "talking" about Hicks in the past seven days. By comparison, the percentage of Starbucks fans that *"were here"* was just one-fourth that of Hicks fans and the percentage of Starbucks fans "talking" about Starbucks was less than one-sixth of what Hicks achieves.

No wonder Hicks Nurseries is 160 years young and growing strong. As the company has no doubt done throughout its history, it is delivering great products and services. Hicks is also using the newest tools to full advantage; in this case, the company is using social media in a way that even the biggest competitors cannot.

If you run a small business, you too have this potential new engagement advantage over your larger competitors. However, if your business is already using Facebook and not getting at least 1% engagement, it's probably time to retool or try something else.

As you think about using Facebook for your business, consider your overall social strategy. You won't be able to use every social media tool. If you sell B2C, however, Facebook could be the right first step.

Why Google+ Is Better Than Facebook for B2B: My Theory

As a rule, Facebook is great if your business sells B2C. You'll find countless great B2C models to review and analyze, starting with Starbucks (www.facebook.com/Starbucks), the most admired brand in social media, and Hicks Nurseries (www.facebook.com/HicksNurseries), the fabulous small-business example described in this chapter. But try to find similarly great (or even adequate) B2B models. They are surprisingly rare.

I've never seen an official explanation for Facebook's poor fit for B2B applications, but I have a theory. In real life (IRL), we have different personal and professional personas. For example, we dress differently for the office than we do for hanging out with friends on weekends.

With Facebook, it's all but impossible to maintain separate personal and professional personas. It seems as though everybody sees everything, and that's the problem. If you sell B2B, consider Google+ instead, because IRL we have different *circles* of friends and professional associates and Google+ embraces and separates these circles. That's sheer genius.

If you're not already a Google+ expert, read about it in Chapter 12.

CHAPTER 11 SUMMARY

❏ With 1.2 billion members, Facebook is the largest social network.

❏ Facebook may be your best social tool if you sell B2C. Other tools may be more valuable than Facebook if you sell B2B.

❏ Facebook offers the opportunity for social dialogue, which helps a business learn about customers and customers learn about the business's products and services.

❏ Facebook's feature that allows a visitor to Like a page results in business "fans" who provide peer endorsements, the most valuable kind of free PR.

❏ As you consider a Facebook initiative, study the Facebook strategies of businesses like yours that have been successful. Learn from their experience.

❏ Utilize one or more of the major drivers of Likes.

- Provide discounts and promotions.

- Offer freebies (e.g., samples).

- Post updates on future products.

- Give updates on future sales.

- Provide fun or entertainment.

- Offer access to exclusive content.

- Provide education about company topics.

- Offer opportunities to interact (i.e., to provide feedback).

❏ Although most big consumer-focused companies already use Facebook, the social network can be even more valuable to small companies. Hicks Nurseries is a great example.

❏ A Facebook Like is only the beginning. To be successful with Facebook, you must fully engage at least 1% of your fans.

CHAPTER 12

GOOGLE+: YOU CAN'T IGNORE THIS ONE

In mid-2011, when Google announced a new social network called Google+ (www.plus.google.com), which is pronounced "Google Plus," my expectations were low. Google was already a three-time loser in social networking. Have you ever heard of Orkut, Wave, or Buzz? I didn't think so.

Based on a poor record of accomplishment, I figured that Google engineers just didn't get social networking, let alone real-world networking. (Hey, I'm an engineer too, so I can make fun of our kind.) My opinion changed when I discovered that more than 10 million people had joined Google+ during the first two weeks. What's more, at the time, you couldn't even sign up; you had to be invited by someone who was already a member. That's genius!

Google is going to succeed at social networking ... or literally die trying, because social represents a fundamental threat to Google's business. Why would I use Google to search for something if I could ask my friends? That's what all of us do on Facebook, the No. 2 (and by some measures, the No. 1) most visited site in the world.

INVESTIGATE THE CIRCLES OF LIFE

Google+ will change Facebook and LinkedIn (evolve or die), and I believe it will change how we do B2B social networking.

My theory about why B2B doesn't work well on Facebook is that on Facebook there's too much cross-bleed of personal and professional.

On Facebook, almost everything you do is shared with everybody you Friend and often with many of their friends. People use Facebook to share their family and personal pursuits, and they don't typically want the same information to be seen by their professional associates. We all have somewhat separate personal and professional personas, and it's best if they remain relatively separate. If you think I'm being too conservative here, I ask you: Do you dress the same for the office as you do at home on weekends?

In real life, we don't share everything with everybody. Instead, we have various circles of personal and professional associates with whom we have different conversations.

Google+ is built on this concept of circles. When you connect with a person on Google+, you indicate which circle that person belongs to. I can have a circle for family, a circle for friends, a circle for employees, and a circle for customers. I can have a circle for any group. Since people don't see what circle (or circles) that they're a part of, I can have a circle for idiots I want to avoid.

Every time you add someone to your Google+ network, Google forces you to assign him or her to one or more circles. Facebook and LinkedIn can't copy this. Oh, they can copy the feature (and Facebook already has), but it doesn't work after people have already built their networks. Virtually no one will take the time to go back and partition his or her monolithic network. It would take too much time or too much thinking, even in the unlikely event that the person understood the potential benefit.

With Google+ circles, each time you post content, you specify which circle or circles of people you want to receive the content. Some things go just to your professional connections. Others go to friends and family. Yet others go exclusively to customers.

Along parallel lines, when you consume content on Google+, you don't have to look at everything from everybody. During the business day, you can focus on the people and content in your employee and customer circles. During evenings and weekends, you can catch up with your family and friends via those circles. This network partitioning is almost as big an idea as social networking itself.

YOU CAN'T IGNORE GOOGLE+

If you were a fan of Google Reader or of my favorite social dashboard, iGoogle (see Chapter 19), you were likely disappointed when Google shut down both. This move was part of Google's strategic pivot to social networking.

The company has rebranded Google Places as Google+ Local and is investing billions in developing new features for Google+. This constitutes an all-out "arms race" against Facebook.

One of my favorite Google+ features to date (I expect many more to follow) is called *Hangout*. This feature allows you to set up a nine-way videoconference free. Imagine the value of that, for example, the next time you want to engage your Customer Service Team in solving a customer service problem.

All of this is compelling, but the real reason you must use Google+ is that, whether you realize it or not, Google brings you customers. As I've mentioned before, half of all Internet traffic starts with a search. Google accounts for more than two-thirds of search volume. You don't want to ignore that opportunity – and, increasingly, the opportunity depends on participating in Google+.

Have you ever googled a business name (e.g., Ruth's Chris Steak House) or, more important, a related word or phrase (e.g., *restaurant*) and noticed that Google often presents a map showing relevant results near your current location? If you haven't tried this lately, check it out now – it's amazing.

If you simply hover your cursor over an associated business listing (no need to even click on it), a photo of the establishment, its address, its business hours, and countless reviews pop up in the right column. You can usually make a reservation right from the Google results page via Google's link to a third party website.

Where does such business data come from? Googlemobiles that drive around photographing and mapping the streets of the world collected some of it. Most of the data, however, was supplied directly by business owners.

As such, it's clear that Google's algorithms make use of, among other data, location data via Google+. We'll look at these factors separately, including the importance of authorship, but there's one more concept to explore first: Google+ business pages.

Create Your Google+ Business Page
(and Remember the Importance of Location)

To quote Google:

> "Think of your Google+ business page as your brand hub. Your page, along with your profile image and recent posts, is eligible to show on the right-hand side of our results when relevant to a customer's search. Relevant posts can also show up within search results for your page's followers."

In other words, play nice with Google+ and Google+ will bring you traffic. Don't participate and maybe not so much.

Before getting started on your own Google+ business page, review some outstanding examples of Google+ pages by accessing http://bit.ly/12r3Sbt, which will take you to a blog post on the website Social Media Delivered. Scanning the QR code will take you to the same destination. You'll find great models from media companies to government organizations to nonprofits, etc.

Scan to see 20
model Google+ pages

The one type of business underrepresented in the blog post is the sector consisting of industrial and B2B companies. Search traffic may be even more important for such entities than for B2C organizations.

To see an outstanding example of how a B2B firm embraces social media and benefits from search, visit www.jfrecycle.com, the website of New England's oldest and largest privately owned scrap metal processor. There are literally 10s of thousands of other B2B examples, but they are hard to find because the sites target specific, narrow audiences, not the public.

Now, with a favorite best-practice model in mind, go to www.plus.google.com. You'll be asked to log in or create an account. Search for your business name and then create or claim your Google+ business page. Google likely already created at least one page for you, whether you wanted it or not. If you find such a page, look for a button like this:

After completing the claiming process (or creating a new page), you'll notice that your business is not yet verified. This is where *location* starts to factor in.

152

HOW CAN I CAPITALIZE ON SOCIAL MEDIA
WHEN MY KID HAS TO PROGRAM MY DVR?

After clicking on the blue Verify now button, you'll be prompted to enter your business address and phone number, among other attributes. To verify that you are located exactly where you say you are, Google uses the postal system to complete the process. Watch your U.S. mail mailbox for a postcard that looks like this:

Your PIN postcard will look something like this:

The card details a simple three-step process for completing your listing. Step 3 involves entering a five-digit PIN, which the card provides. Be careful not to miss the postcard when it shows up in the mail. Google also has a phone-based verification process that is definitely faster.

On your Google+ business home page, add to the footer the addresses of your major business locations. Do the same to the footer of your business contact page. This helps tie everything neatly together from a local search perspective.

For additional assistance with creating and managing your Google+ business pages, visit www.google.com/+/brands/.

EXPLORE GOOGLE+ PERSONAL PAGES
(AND REMEMBER THE IMPORTANCE OF AUTHORSHIP)

Google+ also features personal pages, just as Facebook does. If you followed the process outlined above, you now have a personal page and should begin populating it with content.

On both business and personal pages, there's a small down-arrow in the upper-right area, next to your small photo or profile icon, that allows you to toggle between the two types of pages, as shown here.

Select your personal page if you are not already on it. Here is my personal page:

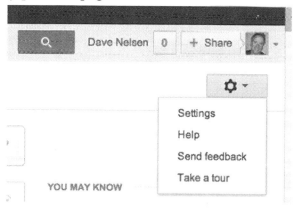

You'll see the Settings icon (it looks like a cog). Next to it is a down-arrowhead that allows you to access a dropdown menu. Select "Take a tour" to learn directly from Google, or select Settings to get started.

From there, you'll have five additional choices. Click on Account and add a professional photo. You can also add one or more email addresses and myriad information. Since doing this is going to help you and your business turn up in search results when people search for information about what you do (without necessarily ever having heard of you), invest a little bit of time.

In addition, I recommend accessing Security and setting up two-step verification so that bad guys can't hijack your account. Add a secondary mobile recovery number in case you lose your phone while traveling. If it's not obvious how (or why) to take these actions, just google "secondary mobile recovery number."

Also review and get comfortable with the default profile and privacy settings and learn how to toggle them on or off as desired.

Now it is time for Google authorship. Remember my earlier advice about PIE? Use personality, along with interesting and entertaining content, to attract attention and build trust. Remember the adage in sales: People buy from people. Google now allows you to link your content to your Google+ profile to *make your content feel personal.* How cool (and important) is that!

To get started, go to https://plus.google.com/authorship and click on the blue Signup for Authorship button.

After that, follow these four simple rules:

1. Make sure you have a profile photo with a recognizable headshot.
2. Make sure a byline containing your name appears on each page of your content.
3. Make sure your byline name matches the name on your Google+ profile.
4. Verify you have an email address on the same domain as your content.

As you create compelling content over time, authorship will help you and your business get found in searches more often. Authorship will also enhance your reputation as an industry thought leader.

Google+ is fabulous, save for one thing: when it was invented. If it had been invented before LinkedIn and Facebook, it would be the only social network we would ever need. Unfortunately, since 200 million professionals already use LinkedIn, we must continue our professional networking there. In addition, with 1.2 billion people on Facebook, we must continue our personal (and consumer-focused) networking there.

Still, Google+ is a force that can't be ignored, especially given the market power and resources of the world's No. 1 search company. So now we have three important social media networks to attend to. As such, B2C social media networking – and more significantly, B2B social media networking – will become ever more functional and valuable. That fact will justify the additional time investment. Google+ will help build trust (which leads to sales) and will help people find your business instantly when they are looking for information about what your business does.

Try These Amazing Google Queries

Type any airline name and flight number. You don't even have to hit Enter or click on anything. The flight status will magically appear.

Google | usairways flight 94|
us **airways** flight 94
us **airways** flight 945
us **airways** flight 949
us **airways** flight 942

Showing results for *us airways* flight 94
Search instead for usairways flight 94

US Airways Flight 94
On-time - departs in 4 hours 29 mins

BOS ✈ ──────────────── • PHX

Departs Boston, today			Arrives Phoenix, today		
Time	Terminal	Gate	Time	Terminal	Gate
4:25 PM	B	B14	7:12 PM	4	A9

Type "define" followed by any word or phrase. The definition will magically appear.

Google | define seo|
define seo
define **seance**
define seo **sem**
define seo **content writing**

seo

Abbreviation
Search engine optimization.

More info -

Search engine optimization - Wikipedia, the free encyclopedia
en.wikipedia.org/wiki/Search_engine_optimization ▾
Search engine optimization (SEO) is the process of affecting the visibility of a website
or a web page in a search ..... "What is a tall poppy among web pages?".
SEO (disambiguation) - Search engine marketing - Backlink - Website promotion

Type any conversion in desired units. I'm currently training for a triathlon involving a 1,500-meter swim. However, I'm training in a pool measured in yards. How many yards should I be swimming?

Google | 1500 meters to yards

Web   Images   Maps   Shopping   More ▾   Search tools

About 7,540,000 results (0.31 seconds)

Length

1500   ═   1640.42

Meter   Yard

Swimming Workouts - Build to 1500 Meters or Yards
swimming.about.com › ... › Build Your Swimming ▾
Want to get swimming workouts going, but think you are a weak swimmer and won't be able to do it? If you can already complete the.

Type in the beginning of any question and review the autocompleted suggestions. They're an interesting mix of practical and weird.

Google | How come my g

how come my google chrome is not working
how come my gums are black
how come my google chrome is slow
how come my girlfriend wont talk to me

Hopefully, your issue is along the lines of a silent girlfriend rather than black gums.

CHAPTER 12 SUMMARY

☐ Google+ is similar to Facebook, except that Google+ is built on the concept of circles. When you connect with a person on Google+, you indicate which circle(s) that person belongs to. You can have any number and manner of circles, including family, friends, customers, employees, etc.

☐ Google+ mimics real life in that it allows you to separate personal and professional personas. As a result, it's a great tool for B2B as well as B2C companies.

☐ You can't afford to ignore Google+, even if you already use LinkedIn and Facebook. You can't ignore Google's power in search, and Google rankings are increasingly tied to participating in Google+.

☐ One of Google's powerful features is a map showing relevant results near the searcher's current location. This could bring you business.

☐ Google Authorship allows you to populate your business and personal pages with content that improves your search results.

☐ While you can't ignore the power of Google+, you can't stop participating in LinkedIn or Facebook. Too many people use these tools.

CHAPTER 13

UNDERSTAND QUICK RESPONSE CODES

By now, you've noticed that I've been using quick response codes (QR codes, or QRCs) throughout this book. If you haven't scanned one of these codes yet, try it now. Get started by adding a QR reader (aka QR scanner) to your smartphone by visiting your appropriate app store and choosing one. Then flip back to the first QR code in Chapter 1 to see Dan Aykroyd's Bass-o-Matic in action.

In 1994 a division of Toyota invented QR codes to track parts and packages. However, the rise of smartphones – which have both a camera and an Internet connection – helped make these codes mainstream.

The purpose of a QR code is to supplement what might be called a person's real-world experience with content delivered via smartphone.

For example, I recently purchased a new lawnmower at Home Depot. When I opened the box to begin setup, I discovered a QR code. Scanning the code, I found a helpful video to speed setup. Watching the video was much better than trying to read a manual. Nobody wants to read when the sun is shining and the grass waits.

In my travels, I see companies use QR codes poorly more often than not. Imagine my disappointment and the inconsiderate waste of my time – if the lawnmower QR code had taken me to Home Depot's home page. Yet some companies do that.

Imagine my frustration if the page I landed on had been a traditional web page perfectly optimized for a 24-inch monitor.

When someone scans your QR code, the one certain thing is that they're looking at a screen whose height is 4–5 inches. Yet all the time companies make the mistake of linking QR codes to targets that aren't optimized for mobile devices.

If you use QR codes, make the result *specific and complementary* to the person's real-world experience and *design the destination site for a mobile screen.*

When and Where Should You Use QR Codes?

In this book you may have noticed that QR codes have appeared in conjunction with some, but not all, URLs. Did you decode the "when and where" logic of my code-inclusion choices?

Use QR codes when

☐ Viewing associated content on a mobile phone makes sense

☐ The URL is inconveniently long and hard to type

In Chapter 1, I used QR codes to show you the Bass-o-Matic video and one of Tom Dixon's Blendtec blender videos. They were relevant to the chapter content and, as videos, they were easy to view on your smartphone as you read this book on a printed page or an Amazon Kindle. (In either case, the videos complemented your text experience.) Actually typing the respective URLs would have been inconvenient, especially in the case of the URL of the Blendtec video: https://m.youtube.com/watch?v=K0m4x0y3QNw (In a link, a zero can be hard to distinguish from the letter *o*.) As for where to use QR codes, that depends on where you can enhance your target audience's real-world experience. I've seen them in many places:

☐ Business cards – to autoload contact information

☐ Product brochures – to provide an associated video that presents a product demonstration or customer testimonial

- ☐ The front door of the Washington Square Hotel, in New York City – to present a short tour of the delightful facility

- ☐ Trade show exhibits – to share product information without cluttering show attendees' bags or killing trees

- ☐ Restaurant menus – to "check in," Follow, or Like

One important rule for using QR codes is that they must be big enough to appear as roughly a 1-inch square on a smartphone screen. At the Steel Cactus restaurant, in Pittsburgh, the two QR codes on the menu are so small that even when I hold my phone within ¼ inch of the menu, the codes won't scan. On countless billboards, unless I jump some fences and climb the structure, I won't be close enough to scan the codes. And don't get me started on QR codes on 18 wheelers. Since most people encounter the trucks when traveling at 55 miles per hour on a freeway, are they trying to get us killed?

LEARN TO GENERATE QR CODES

QR codes are regulated by several international standards organizations. According to Wikipedia, one of the oldest (dating to October 1997) is AIM (Association for Automatic Identification and Mobility).

Many dozens of websites generate QR codes free or at a low cost. I've used the free code generator from QR Stuff (www.qrstuff.com) to generate the codes included in this book. Try code generation yourself. It's *copy* (your target URL) – *paste – download* easy.

One potential problem with QR codes is their granularity. Oversimplifying a bit (ignoring error correction, data compression, etc.), you can think of a QR code as a binary number in which a black square represents a 0 and a white square represents a 1. Eight such squares together represent a number from 0 to 255. Each number corresponds to a character: 65 represents A; 66, B; and so on.

Short URLs require fewer black and white squares to encode, so they can be bigger and easier to scan. If you have
long URLs, which are not uncommon, you'll need many
squares to encode the addresses. Here's an example. I once
titled a blog post in such a way that the URL of the post was

http://dialogconsulting.com/best-market-research-
learning-about-any-industry-using-linkedin/

Using a link-shortening service, http://www.bit.ly, I transformed that link into this link: http://bit.ly/T1NnFx

Encoding the two URLs into QR codes will allow scan-
ners to reach the same destination, but which one do you think
is easier for a scanner to resolve?

Scan to see a long URL and a short URL in action

The bottom line: Test your QR code before you print it on
10,000 brochures.

One last thing: It's a good idea to tell people why they
should scan your code. If the reason is one of clear and compelling value to them, you'll get much better utilization. Put a
naked QR code out there and most people will just ignore it.

CHAPTER 13 SUMMARY

☐ Use free QR codes to engage your audience.

☐ Create QR codes at the QR Stuff website or another website that generates QR codes.

☐ Use such codes when the associated content is best presented on a mobile phone and when URLs would be hard to type.

☐ Tell people why they should scan your QR code.

☐ Design the destination site for a mobile screen.

☐ Make the result specific and complementary to a person's real-world situation.

☐ Test a QR code before printing it on collateral material.

CHAPTER 14

BUSINESS BLOG:
FOR LOW-TECH, GET A HIGH RETURN

Blogging is perhaps the most accessible form of social media. A blog is essentially a website with one additional feature, the ability for the readers to add comments if they desire. (For an in-depth definition of *blog,* see Wikipedia at http://en.wikipedia.org/wiki/Blog.) Therefore, any demographic group already comfortable online will likely be comfortable reading a blog. Blogging is relatively low-tech compared with other forms of social media.

The word *blog* is a contraction of the term *web log.* A blog contains regular entries, or posts, including commentary, audio, video, and/or graphics. Blog entries are displayed in chronological order, with the newest post displayed first (at the top). A reader can access previous entries by scrolling or by clicking on a menu of categories on the blog site.

You might think of blogs as online newspapers produced by regular people for their own personal or professional purposes. Unlike a newspaper, however, a blog is rarely written about many topics and for a mass audience. Instead, most blogs focus narrowly on a specific topic, industry, product line, person, or passion. As a rule, narrowly focused content works best in social media.

Although some social media initiatives cost more to deliver than they generate in return, if you follow a few simple rules, blogging is all but guaranteed to show a positive return on investment (ROI). That's because *companies that blog generate 55% more web traffic, on average, than those that*

166

How Can I Capitalize on Social Media
When My Kid Has to Program My DVR?

don't. (Find this marketing statistic and more at http://blog.hubspot.com/blog/tabid/6307/bid/11414/12-Mind-Blowing-Statistics-Every-Marketer-Should-Know.aspx, a posting on the HubSpot website (http://blog.hubspot.com/).

If your website works to convert visitors to customers, 55% more web traffic will translate directly to your bottom line. How and why do blogs generate traffic?

Half of all Internet traffic starts with a search. Today there will be roughly three billion searches. Tomorrow there will be three billion searches. Two-thirds of these searches will be Google searches.

Nobody can tell you exactly how Google works because the company changes its algorithms roughly 500 times per year. In late 2011, Google made the single biggest change ever, to favor newer content over older. Today, if you have a static website, your site is falling in the Google rankings. If you blog regularly about topics of interest to your target audience, you're rising in the Google rankings. So companies that blog generate 55% more web traffic.

More important, the traffic generated by blogging is not random traffic. No, blogging brings 55% more searchers who find you at the precise moment they are looking for information about what you do. As a result, blogging is an ideal social media starting point for most businesses and organizations.

Two other benefits of blogging are perhaps even more important than additional web traffic. When done effectively:

1. Blogging positions you as an expert in your field. This perceived expertise bestows a media halo upon you and your company.

2. Blogging builds trust. As you know, trust is the foundation of any sale. Blogging helps you build trust on a scale that can't be achieved through in-person contact.

Blogging also allows you to connect with your audience members over both time and distance. When written in a timeless and educational manner, every new blog post is compelling content for current and countless future readers. You can interact with them via their comments, independent of geography, whether they are readers today or in the future. Blogging provides this classic "long tail" benefit.

If you're already producing a periodic newsletter or email blast, you may already have relevant content for your blog. Most newsletters and email blasts have the shelf life of lettuce as they roll through people's mail- and Inboxes (not that I have anything against lettuce). By putting your content online, its shelf life is dramatically extended, thanks to Google.

Finally, blogging is more controllable (a word I am loath to use when talking about *conversations*) than other forms of social media. Unlike with other social media services, you approve or block blog readers' comments on a case-by-case basis. (Block sparingly.)

If blogging sounds interesting, get started by reading and analyzing a few outstanding blogs as models. Some of my favorite examples follow, with short explanations that tell why I like each case so much.

CASE STUDY 1: *RANDY'S JOURNAL*

I first mentioned *Randy's Journal* (www.BoeingBlogs.com/randy) in Chapter 3, where I explained that Randy is vice president of marketing, Boeing Commercial Airplanes. Due to its very small but very important audience, *Randy's Journal* is likely one of the most valuable B2B blogs on the planet.

Even though Boeing is a multibillion-dollar company, it's not a faceless corporation; it's Randy. In a blog, it's a great idea to feature your people using their real names (first name only) and their pictures. This creates a sense of connection that builds trust.

Be careful, however, to avoid painting yourself into the same corner that Boeing did. Don't brand the whole blog after an individual who might leave or retire. The original Randy did exactly that (retired) and Boeing had a problem. Everybody in the airline industry knew *Randy's Journal.* Now what do you do? "Hey, everybody, meet Larry. It's now *Larry's Journal.* Get used to the new name."

That's not what Boeing did in this true-life case study. Instead, the company sent an email to the Executive Team. "Does anybody know anybody named Randy who can write?" The guy pictured above raised his hand, and on they went with Randy 2.

I recommend that you attach the author's name and picture to his or her individual posts and involve multiple contributors (potentially, even customers). Name the blog more generally – for example, *The Boeing Journal* or *The Airline Executive Insider.*

If you look up the statistics (see how in Chapter 21), you'll see that Randy averages roughly 10,000 monthly readers. Why would such a small audience be of interest and value to such a large company? Well, Randy is not writing for people who fly on Boeing planes; Randy is writing for people who can *buy* Boeing planes – airline industry executives. Even small audiences can be incredibly valuable.

Read a few of Randy's posts. Ask yourself if the posts are valuable to people who buy airplanes. And look for the concept of PIE: personality, interesting, and entertaining. You'll understand how blog posts can build trust, the kind that leads to sales.

CASE STUDY 2: *MED LAW BLOG*

I am often asked, "Can professional services firms benefit from social media?" To answer I offer the example of a professional services organization on the small end of the B2B company-size spectrum, Tucker Arensberg, a law firm with roughly 75 attorneys. The firm's #1 source of inbound business is the *Med Law Blog* (www.MedLawBlog.com/). Michael A. Cassidy is the writer and publisher.

As you review *Med Law Blog,* consider how the blog's approach is effective for lawyers, doctors, accountants, and most small and medium-sized B2B companies.

Like the best blogs, *Med Law Blog* creates a sense of connection with a person (or persons). In this case, it's Michael. But as with Randy and Boeing, I don't advise branding your blog after one individual.

That aside, consider the value proposition of *Med Law Blog* for the target audience. With the advent of Obamacare (aka the Patient Protection and Affordable Care Act), business leaders have countless questions and concerns about health care benefits and compliance.

Along comes Michael, who writes about

- ☐ Compliance
- ☐ Electronic health records
- ☐ Employee benefits
- ☐ Fraud
- ☐ The Health Insurance Portability and Accountability Act (HIPAA)
- ☐ Medicare and reimbursement

Notice that Michael is not giving away his services as free advice in his blog. Rather, he's alerting people to issues they need to understand. In so doing, Michael is demonstrating his expertise and establishing himself as a trusted adviser. Is it really a surprise that the firm's #1 source of inbound business is the *Med Law Blog?*

By the way, human psychology is such that – when people give us something, including valuable information – we look for ways to reciprocate. People look for ways to become Michael's customer. This is what inbound marketing looks like. And from the great folks at HubSpot (mentioned earlier), we know that inbound marketing costs 62% less than outbound marketing.

Whenever Michael is writing a blog post rather that working on a client project, he's no doubt giving up hundreds of dollars per hour. Even if this adds up to 10s of thousands of dollars per year, dollars to donuts says that his blog produces an impressive ROI for his firm.

Still *Med Law Blog* has room for improvement. (I offered my observations to Tucker Arensberg this morning, as unsolicited free advice via email.)

The *Med Law Blog* lives in its own domain, www.MedLawBlog.com. As such, blog traffic doesn't directly benefit the main website, www.TuckerLaw.com, from a search perspective. Why fracture search engine optimization (SEO) resources across multiple domains, causing everything in both domains to rank lower in search results? Ideally, the *Med Law*

Blog should be part of www.TuckerLaw.com. (but this link doesn't exist)

In my email to Tucker Arensberg, I highlighted another shortcoming – one I've seen all too frequently. From an SEO perspective, the firm's URLs are flawed and represent a missed opportunity. A typical web page address at the Tucker Arensberg website begins with www.TuckerLaw.com and ends with a lot of characters that are meaningless to most humans. The characters are like this: secondary.aspx?id=7&p=0.

In search, the characters that appear after the domain name are very important. They are valuable when it comes to getting found.

Your page addresses should contain the most significant keywords related to that page's content. Remember, half of all Internet traffic starts with a search. Some fraction of the three billion searches run today will be by people looking for information about what you do. You want to be found.

CASE STUDY 3: *SHARING MAYO CLINIC*

In a world of HIPAA and patient privacy, you'd think that blogging by a medical provider would be all but impossible. And you'd be wrong.

The same can be said for financial advisers constrained by FINRA (Financial Industry Regulatory Authority) and teachers governed by FERPA (Family Educational Rights and Privacy Act).

It's possible to blog even in highly regulated industries, because nothing happens on your blog without your approval. That's true even for the comments. For example, look at the blog *Sharing Mayo Clinic* (http://sharing.mayoclinic.org/).

Patient Care   Health   MAYO   For Medical   Research   Education
                Information   CLINIC   Professionals

Request an Appointment   Find a Doctor   Find a Job   Log In to Patient Account   Give to Mayo Clinic

Sharing Mayo Clinic
Stories from patients, family, friends and Mayo Clinic staff

Notice that *Sharing Mayo Clinic* does not brand itself around a single person. Instead, it has a nice clean header that tells you exactly what's it's about: "Stories from patients, family, friends, and Mayo Clinic staff."

The blog gets personal with photos of people in virtually every post (two examples shown below).

The URL of the website is http://Sharing.MayoClinic.org. The URL of the blog is www.MayoClinic.org/sharing. As you

see, the domain names are very similar. Both are helpful in guiding a reader and a search to the blog.

I like how this blog microsegments its audience by allowing a reader to choose an interest by means of the Categories drop-down menu, as follows.

Categories

✓ Select Category
Alternative Medicine (1)
Amenities (60)
Cancer (168)
Cardiology & Cardiac Surgery (70)
Development (8)
Diabetes & Endocrinology (2)
Education (20)
ENT/Audiology (19)
Events (62)
Gastroenterology (20)
General Internal Medicine (4)

Think about the value proposition for an audience of healthcare patients. If you come down with some new condition tomorrow, wouldn't it be compelling to connect with others on that same journey, in an environment curated by the Mayo Clinic? Indeed!

At the same time, you are unlikely to care about all diseases. I, for one, try not to read about a disease I don't have, because I'll mysteriously experience its symptoms.

Another benefit of using categories is that any post can be tagged with one or more, thereby allowing it to appear in multiple places without being replicated. That beats the heck out of the old hierarchical filing systems.

FIND OUT WHAT'S HAPPENING BEFORE YOU START BLOGGING

Before you start writing a blog, find out what's happening in your industry. Find a model blog from which you can learn:

Read an existing blog that is already connecting with its (your) target audience. With 200+ million blogs out there, and with the number growing, there's guaranteed to be one. More likely, there are dozens that exactly match your interests, no matter how narrow, specialized, or esoteric.

To find a blog in your field of interest, you could use Google Blog Search (www.google.com/blogsearch). I prefer Technorati (www.technorati.com), the self-described "leading blog search engine and most comprehensive source of information on the blogosphere." Among other factors, Technorati considers keywords, tags, and what Technorati calls the authority of the writer – essentially, that person's influence with a given audience.

On the Technorati website, in the box labeled "Search for blogs," type a word or phrase that best describes your industry or business interest. For example, enter "Architect" and you will receive 827 results.

Pick one with an authority score in the triple digits (scores range 1–999, with higher being better) and you'll be likely to find a credible and successful blogger-architect.

Find a credible blogger in your field and observe how he or she creates visibility. Interact by commenting, remembering to follow the Cocktail Party Rule. Like the blogger you are using as a model, you may be able to draw people to you based on your insights and expertise.

Before You Start Blogging, Remember One More Thing

There's one other thing to do before you start blogging or assigning a group of people in your organization to do so. Remember Chapter 7 and the 11-step process of planning a social media initiative? Yes, complete those steps. Document each in writing, so you have a plan.

To illustrate, I'll share a personal example. I write a blog, http://dialogconsulting.com/social-media-for-business-blog/, to help business executives successfully apply social media tools in their companies. Here's a glimpse at my own social media plan.

Target Audience(s)

Executives and leaders of small and medium-sized businesses who may want to engage me as their social media consultant, and event planners for industry associations and corporate meetings who may be interested in booking me as a keynote speaker or trainer for their next event.

Value Provided

Informative, educational, and actionable information including tips, how to's, best practices, real-world examples, and case studies about social media and social networking for business.

By sharing relevant information with my target audiences, while not overtly marketing or selling, I keep myself top of mind and perfectly positioned to connect when they need help with their company's social media strategy. Other people may become readers and subscribers, and that's not a problem. Who knows where those connections will lead?

CHOOSE THE BEST BLOGGING PLATFORM

There are many blogging platforms to choose from. For business applications, I recommend using WordPress (www.WordPress.com). It is a free feature-rich hosted service used by 10s of thousands of businesses in every industry segment.

To get started, do *not* go to www.WordPress.com and click on the orange "Sign up now" button to create your company's account. Instead, for maximum search engine optimization (SEO) benefit, get your own installation of WordPress. You can do that at any hosting provider – for example, www.godaddy.com/hosting/wordpress-hosting.aspx. It will likely cost you just a few dollars per month.

To connect your domain name with your blog name, as discussed earlier in this chapter, I recommend moving your whole website to WordPress. That can be done after you start your blog. Don't let a long list of to do's keep you from taking the first steps.

When you're ready to create your first blog, follow these instructions:

1. Log in to your account at your hosting provider and access WordPress.

2. You should land on your WordPress dashboard. If not, on the left-hand side, beneath your blog name, click on the Dashboard button.

3. In the left-hand column, click on Posts (to expand the Posts list) and then click Add New in that sub-list.

4. The cursor will be positioned in the Title field. Type a title for your new blog post.

5. Use the Tab key or mouse to move to the next field. Enter the text of your blog post. Notice the familiar formatting buttons for bold, italics, and underlining; color and text size; and spell-checker. There's even a handy Paste from Word function for those who have drafted text by using Microsoft Word. Note that the rightmost button on the top line provides access to additional formatting options.

6. Also notice buttons to upload or insert images, video, and audio, as well as a button to create a poll. These features add life and color to plain text.

7. When finished (and periodically while in progress) click the Save Draft button and then the Preview button, both in the upper-right area. This will open a new window with a preview of the finished product. Close this window to return to the editing window. Next, add some tags to help new people discover this post. On the right side, in the box labeled

Post Tags, type some words or phrases, separated by commas that broadly describe the content of this specific post. For example, if this chapter were a blog post, I might use the following tags: social networking, social media, blogging, business, WordPress. Click on the Add button when finished.

8. Finally, on the right side, click on the Publish button. Just above that button, notice that the default is "publish immediately." You can set publishing for a future date and time if desired.

9. Should you need to modify or delete this post in the future, execute the first three steps above to access the Edit Posts screen. Hover your cursor over the title of the post and you'll see choices to edit, delete, or view the post. Also note the buttons that will allow you to see statistics and comments regarding that post.

Be sure to post regularly, meaning somewhere between once a month and a few times per week. Like Goldilocks, your readers will enjoy the "just right" amount of content; not too little and not too much. Like you, they have busy lives and want concise, high-quality information that helps them in their pursuits. Too much information is overwhelming. Overwhelm them and they'll disengage.

Remember, marketing is not about you; it's about them. What could you blog about that is about them? Answer that question and you're on your way.

Congratulations, you're now officially a blogger!

Chapter 14 Summary

☐ A blog is essentially a website with one additional feature, the ability for the readers to add comments if they desire. The word *blog* is a contraction of the term *web log*. A blog contains regular entries, or posts, including commentary, audio, video, and/or graphics. Blog entries are displayed in chronological order, with the newest post displayed first (at the top). A reader can access previous entries by scrolling or by clicking on a menu of categories on the blog site.

☐ Most blogs focus on a specific topic, industry, product line, person, or passion.

☐ According to HubSpot, companies that blog generate 55% more web traffic, on average, than those that don't.

☐ Blogging brings relevant traffic to your site. It also allows you to brand yourself as an expert while building trust with your target-audience members.

☐ Before starting a blog, review your social media plan to make sure a blog fits your strategy. Next find blogs in your industry by using Technorati. Learn from those blogs.

☐ Post regularly but not so often that you overwhelm your readers.

CHAPTER 15

GETSATISFACTION:
IMPROVE CUSTOMER SATISFACTION
THE EASY WAY

Yes, you *can* GetSatisfaction. More important, so can your customers. Okay, what exactly *is* GetSatisfaction?

In Chapter 5, I touched on how Zappos and my own company, TalkShoe, use a product called GetSatisfaction (GetSat) (https://getsatisfaction.com), to deliver outstanding customer support. I cited these amazing statistics:

- ❏ A reduction of 89% in customer support load, meaning your customer support load can be 1/10 its current level.

- ❏ An increased sense of customer community (The happiest, most knowledgeable customers are the ones who participate.).

- ❏ Improved customer satisfaction scores.

Where else in business could you cut your cost by a factor of 10 and get better results? You can see why GetSat is one of my favorite social media tools.

UNDERSTAND HOW GETSAT WORKS

GetSatisfaction is a cloud-based service embedded into your website, ideally on your Help page. The service allows your customers to type questions in everyday language. GetSat searches your specific database to see if a customer's question (or a similar one) has been asked and answered. In fact, GetSat doesn't even wait until a question is fully formed. As a cus-

tomer types, it suggests relevant questions for which it already
has answers.

More often than not, customers discover their question in
the list of suggestions. The customers click on the question
and find the associated answer. You can see the advantage in
this, and it gets even better.

If a question has not been asked before, it is posted for
other customers to answer. Amazingly often, customers often
pitch in with an answer – because people like to share what
they know.

When a new question is asked and answered by another
customer, the company reviews the answer to approve, modify, or reject it. As a result, the growing collection of answers
stays accurate even as the *crowd* generates much of the content. *Once again, none of us is as smart as all of us.*

When an existing answer doesn't completely address a
customer's question, that customer can add a follow-on question. As a result, your answer trees get bigger and more nu-
anced over time.

Roughly 10% of the time, questions will be complex
enough that your Support Team will still have to answer. But
seriously, it's just 10%. Is there any other area in business
where you can get other people to do 90% of the work for
you? That's why GetSat is one of my favorite social products.

To experience GetSat in action, go to TalkShoe's website:
www.talkshoe.com/blog/index.php/help. Once there, type a
question in the space provided at Step B.

GET STARTED WITH GETSAT

Before TalkShoe started using GetSat, in late 2007, just after
GetSat debuted, we were using an email-based trouble-ticket
system, and handling many phone calls as well. Phone calls
are expensive.

After signing up for GetSat (which was free back then),
we stopped using the trouble-ticket system and started direct-

ing customers' questions through GetSat instead. Since the database was initially empty, things looked pretty much the same in the beginning. We still had to answer nearly every question submitted. With each answer, however, we were slowly adding to the knowledge base.

A few weeks later, we realized we already had a web page with carefully written FAQs – frequently asked questions. We decided to leave our FAQ page online, since some people prefer this option. In addition, we had one of our techies chop the FAQs into individual Qs and As and load them into GetSat. (If you decide to adopt GetSat, you'll want to add your FAQs at the outset.)

After roughly two months, as the answers in the database grew, we began experiencing something delightful: happier customers and a lower support load. At that point, we took the final step. We started encouraging our customers to share their knowledge about using our service with others.

GetSat operates much like a technical forum in which anyone can contribute to a discussion. All the while, the company oversees the conversation, rejecting bad answers and spam, approving good answers, and *promoting* (aka highlighting) the best answers.

As the CEO of TalkShoe, I found using GetSat particularly satisfying because every customer interaction was adding information to our knowledge base. We looked at the questions that were asked (accessed) most often and enhanced the answers. We added additional details, screenshots, and sometimes even videos (see the sidebar in this chapter).

Perhaps you're thinking that overseeing the GetSat conversation and content enhancement are going to eat up the time you save in reduced support cost. Your team will spend a little bit of time doing that, but in my experience (and most likely in the experience of the 70,000 other companies using GetSat) overseeing and enhancing take surprisingly little time. Use a light hand.

Remember, with GetSat you don't just save time; you build community and improve your customer satisfaction results.

GetSat works just as well for B2B companies as it does for B2C companies. The service is also effective for nonprofit organizations. Some companies even use it in a closed, private mode to build and share knowledge among employees. I once met a CEO who was using GetSat among his employees to answer questions about the company's benefits plan, especially the company's evolving health care options.

ACHIEVE HIGHER CUSTOMER SATISFACTION

Let's return to the example of Zappos, mentioned in Chapter 5. In July 2013, I toured Zappos' headquarters in Las Vegas, Nevada, something anyone can do by registering on the company website. If you have even a passing interest in customer service and corporate culture excellence, I recommend this tour. Zappos is simply unbelievable.

On the tour, I noticed a wall where Zappos tracks the company's customer satisfaction scores. These are shared openly with all employees and, apparently, guests (including vendors, partners, and random tourists like me).

Like many companies, Zappos uses a system called Net Promoter Score (NPS) to measure and monitor customer satisfaction. For most companies, it's a challenge to achieve an NPS of 0. A score of 0 means your customers are essentially neutral, or *indifferent,* which is not a good thing in a world of mouth. An NPS of 50 identifies you as *best in class* in virtually any industry. The number on the wall at Zappos that day was above 90. That's astounding!

To read more about Zappos and how the company uses NPS, check out this blog post: www.netpromoter.com/ netpromoter_community/blogs/jeanne_bliss/2010/09/10/how-zappos-does-nps.

Scan to read about customer
satisfaction at Zappos

If you're looking for a place to start a customer satisfaction improvement program (a critically important task in a social media world), a measurement system such as Net Promoter Score – along with GetSat – may be a good first step.

Make Powerful Tutorials for Your Website
By Using Screen-Capture Software

As you seek to support customers and answer their questions, visual tutorials can help you communicate clearly, in cases where mere words would add confusion.

Countless screen-capture tools are available to make producing a product tutorial easy. You can produce such a tutorial right on your desktop. As you walk through the steps and clicks to execute any action, you can record your entire PC or Mac screen or any part of it. The recording can include cursor movements (or not), keyboard input, audio or video content, and even live voiceover from an external microphone (built into many systems, but easy to add if not). Screen capture is the fastest, simplest, and most powerful way to create a user tutorial.

Dozens of screen-capture programs are available, and I have experience with just a handful. I recommend Camtasia Studio (www.techsmith.com/camtasia.html?gclidO=CPvdvJGC_8ACFS1n7Aod9yIADg), from Tech-Smith, for Windows users and Snapz Pro X (www.ambrosiasw.com/utilities/snapzprox/),
from Ambrosia Software, for Mac users.

I find these tools are great for building killer presentations as well as for making tutorials. Why describe something with a boring bulleted list in a PowerPoint show when you can demonstrate it in action through a series of pictures and videos? As a friend's sixth-grade English teacher said, "Don't tell me about the old lady screaming; show me the old lady screaming." Great advice.

CHAPTER 15 SUMMARY

- ☐ Using GetSatisfaction (GetSat) can reduce your customer support load by roughly 90% while improving customer satisfaction scores and creating a sense of customer community.

- ☐ GetSat is useful for B2Cs, B2Bs, nonprofits, and even internal applications.

- ☐ At the time of this writing, 70,000+ companies have adopted GetSat to improve their customer support processes.

- ☐ Give a boost to the GetSat knowledge base by adding your own FAQs to the knowledge base at the time you integrate GetSat into your website.

- ☐ As you learn which GetSat answers your customers access most frequently, use what you learn from customers to enhance those answers.

- ☐ Your customers have experience using your products and are typically delighted to share that knowledge. Invite them to participate.

CHAPTER 16

LIVE PODCASTING: ACHIEVE CUSTOMER INTIMACY AND BUSINESS SUCCESS

Few business leaders would argue with this dictum: The better you know your customers, the better you can serve them, and the more successful your business is likely to be.

When I dropped in on the front lines of customer service at my company, TalkShoe, answering phone calls or handling the toughest GetSat queries, the experience helped me understand my customers' perspectives.

However, starting in August 2006 and continuing until April 2009, I did something even more valuable every other week. (In 2009, I moved on to pursue my next start-up.)

As I mentioned in Chapter 4, I held a live podcast (at TalkShoe we called them talkcasts). I invited everyone who used our service to connect with me live or after the fact. Imagine the value I received by talking to a large group of my customers 26 times a year.

The podcasts not only built my knowledge base, they dramatically increased my customers' satisfaction with TalkShoe. This became clear when we invited our customers to rate us (aka *me*) on our effectiveness in connecting to and communicating with them. On a 5-point scale, our average rating across our entire history was 4.68. That is amazing, given that the rating included everything good and not so good that ever happened!

Typical customer comments (edited for grammar) included:

> User *ranchexit:* I've been chasing around the so-called
> podcast hosting companies for months (and months).
> Without exception, no one takes the time to explain
> their system or process – they leave it up to a website
> or forums to guide you. This talkcast is a perfect ex-
> ample of how it should be done – great info and in-
> struction from a man and company who walk their
> talk(shoe). Dave wants us to know what's going on. He
> also explains it in terms the average Joe (or Jane) can
> understand – no techno gibberish. If you don't know
> your RSS from a hole in the ground – or an FTP from
> your BVDs – this is the place to be. Thanks and "hats
> off" to Dave Nelsen and the TalkShoe team.

> User *randulo:* No matter how big the Internet is (and
> it's big!), the folks at TalkShoe are the best on the
> Web. The whole TalkShoe community can be proud
> that, from the top of the TalkShoe management down
> to the most modest talkcaster like me, they're all
> there to help. Great job, Dave, and all of you.

What's a Podcast, or Talkcast?

The term *podcast* combines *broadcast* and *pod.* A podcast is a
digital presentation made to be consumed in live or recorded
form on an iPod (or iPhone, Droid, etc.) or computer. For my
purposes, I'm talking about audio podcasts. A talkcast is the
same thing as a podcast.

When thinking about audio content, consider this unique
benefit: Busy people can listen to audio content while doing
other things. You can listen to audio while driving, exercising,
mowing the lawn, etc. That's not true of video or text content.
Audio content allows users to multiply time.

What's a Live Interactive Podcast?

There are hundreds of ways to create a podcast. If you have a
digital recorder or digital recording software, such as Garage-
Band (www.apple.com/mac/garageband/), you can record a

conversation among one or more local participants and publish it as a podcast.

However, two notable services allow you to record a podcast while involving live participants from anywhere on the planet and streaming the resulting audio on the Internet. These services include BlogTalkRadio (www.BlogTalkRadio.com/) and TalkShoe (http://TalkShoe.com). Using any of these services, you can create live podcasts with multiple participants calling in via phone or voice over IP (aka VoIP) from their computers. *Think of these podcasts as conference calls on steroids.* Each of these services is free in its basic version.

With TalkShoe, up to 300 people can call in to a live talkcast. Literally thousands more can listen to the live audio stream online.

To avoid chaos, everything is under host control, just like on a radio talk show. The host can do the following:

- ❏ Control whether the talkcast is public or by invitation only
- ❏ Start and end recording
- ❏ Mute and unmute callers (Callers use a "raise hand" signal to indicate the desire to talk.)
- ❏ Text chat with callers
- ❏ Block caller text chat on a per-person basis
- ❏ And more

BENEFIT FROM VALUE AFTER THE FACT

Recordings of a podcast can be available after the fact. Better yet, if someone subscribes to a podcast using an RSS feed (see Chapter 19), every new recording is delivered to him or her automatically, just as a new magazine is delivered to a subscriber. This allows busy people to choose when they listen to your talkcast.

At TalkShoe, for every live talkcast participant, we had roughly 20 after-the-fact listeners. We considered these "long tail" listeners. Even if such listeners rarely participated live, I often heard from them through comments (available on the talkcast page), email, or other method. The input was invaluable.

CASE STUDY: PODCASTING WITH CUSTOMERS ON TALKSHOE

There are a thousand possible uses for BlogTalkRadio and TalkShoe. In fact, when you visit TalkShoe, you can browse 26 different content categories. Most categories contain more than 1,000 separate topics, equating to more than three-quarters of a million recordings to date.

During the time I was hosting talkcasts on TalkShoe, I went live every other Thursday at 4 p.m. Eastern Time, permitting participation across the United States and Canada. After thanking the participants for joining in, I gave a short update on our service enhancements during the previous two weeks. I frequently acknowledged our most successful *hosts* (our term for content creators). With their permission, I shared their best practices with others. Once again, *none of us is as smart as all of us.*

With that section of the program completed, I opened my talkcast to anyone who wanted to ask a question, make a comment, or just talk. Can you imagine a better way to understand customers' concerns, their likes, or their perceived needs? These conversations gave us an incredible advantage. The same technology is easily accessible to you.

Perhaps the single biggest benefit to the company (and to our customers) was enhanced understanding of the features our customers wanted and valued. This understanding allowed me (and our product manager, Aaron Brauser) to make better decisions about allocating TalkShoe's most valuable resource, our engineering cycles (the time it took software engineers to implement new product features). Our customers had countless ideas we hadn't thought of. Indeed, customers live in the real world, and there are more of them than of us. *None of us is as smart as all of us.*

Here's a simple example of one such idea: Talkcasts typically happen at scheduled times. However, TalkShoe provides the option Right Now, which allows a talkcast to occur immediately. The visual below shows the screen a user sees when scheduling an episode, or talkcast. Notice that the default choice for scheduling is Future.

When we first launched TalkShoe, the scheduling screen defaulted to Right Now. In talkcasts, customers told us that a problem resulted from the default setting. Customers said that, after reaching the scheduling screen, they focused on the title and description of their new episode, without attending to the scheduling option. Clicking on the Next button would cause the episode to go live immediately, although that was not what the user intended.

Changing the system default to Future made it impossible for users to make this mistake. Now if a user clicks on the Next button without attending to scheduling, the system reminds him or her to set a date and time. If a user intends to start the call right now, it's easy to select that option.

A simple software change, at nominal cost, made it impossible for our customers to make what had been an annoying and time-consuming mistake. Chances are we would never have noticed the need for the change had we not been talking to our customers every other Thursday at 4 p.m.

How many such opportunities exist in your business? Just think: Enough minor usability enhancements and you have the iPhone, instead of everything that came before.

What If the Talk Is Negative or Proprietary?

Podcasting with customers is valuable, but it's also incredibly open. Perhaps certain problems or risks have already come to mind. What happens when somebody is unhappy or critical? What if your competitors are listening?

I ask you: If someone were unhappy with your company, would you rather learn it sooner, later, or never? Although it may be uncomfortable discovering dissatisfaction in a public forum, the venue gives you a chance to address the issue. Further, it gives you a chance to demonstrate to others how responsive you are. In the process, you learn and improve.

Studies reveal that a customer who has a problem that is satisfactorily resolved will have a longer relationship with your company than a customer who never has a problem. Feedback about problems gives you the chance to turn critics into raving fans.

Regarding competitors listening in, well, that probably happens. But in many cases the content is irrelevant to them (as in the example above, where we changed the scheduling default from Right Now to Future). Even if competitors occasionally glean a new idea or competitive concept, your organization is learning much faster than theirs. I'm willing to accept the tradeoffs.

Be Aware of Other Applications of Podcasting

The possible applications of podcasting with the public are virtually unlimited. I like using the technology in a private mode to connect with my Executive Team. I like my sales VP to use the technology to connect with the Sales Team. Podcasts can be recorded and delivered automatically (via RSS) to the smartphones of people who missed the scheduled podcast or want to re-listen.

Podcasts represent a communication tool that has evolved. Compare the communication tools you are using now. Does it make sense to replace an old tool with this new one?

194   HOW CAN I CAPITALIZE ON SOCIAL MEDIA
                                  WHEN MY KID HAS TO PROGRAM MY DVR?

CREATE YOUR OWN PUBLIC OR PRIVATE PODCAST

Podcasting can be free. Here are the basic steps to get started on TalkShoe, the service with which I am most familiar:

1. Go to www.TalkShoe.com and click on the white Signup button in the header. On subsequent visits, you'll use the credentials you establish during your first visit to sign in to the service.

2. Next click on the green Create button and follow the steps. Initially, you'll create a new call series and then you'll schedule a call episode within that series.

3. Choose a name for your talkcast, or call, series. Specify whether it will be public or unlisted (aka by invitation only) and whether you want the call to be recorded. Regarding recording, the Manual mode allows you to start and end recording at will; Automatic mode starts recording when you call in and terminates recording when you hang up.

4. Finally, select Start Now or Schedule to determine when to start the talkcast.

5. When you are ready to connect, if you are not already on your call page, click on the white myTalkShoe button in the header and select one of the two modes to start your talkcast. One mode works in your browser; the other is a downloadable software application.

For more details on TalkShoe, access tutorial videos and an interactive help system at www.talkshoe.com/blog/index.php/help.

CHAPTER 16 SUMMARY

☐ The term *podcast* combines *broadcast* and *pod*. A podcast is a digital media presentation made to be listened to on an iPod (or iPhone, Droid, etc.) or computer. This chapter discussed audio podcasts (which TalkShoe calls talkcasts).

☐ Audio content is different from video and text in that the user can combine listening with other activities (driving, mowing the lawn, etc.).

☐ In a live interactive podcast, you can record the podcast while involving live participants from anywhere on the planet and streaming the resulting audio on the Internet. You can think of a podcast as a conference call on steroids. Basic versions of podcasting are free at BlogTalkRadio and TalkShoe.

☐ Interactive podcasts allow you to connect to and communicate with customers. Podcasts enable you to deliver content to customers while learning their concerns, likes, and perceived needs.

☐ Interactive podcasts can be used in a private mode to connect with internal team members.

☐ A live podcast can be recorded for future listening. The recordings are then available for use by others, providing a "long tail" benefit.

☐ When a listener subscribes to a podcast via RSS feed, that listener receives new podcasts automatically.

CHAPTER 17

NING:
GIVE YOUR EMPLOYEES A PRIVATE
FACEBOOK-LIKE NETWORK

When was the last time you sent a telegram, used a pager, or even sent a fax? Chances are you've done none of these things recently because communication tools have evolved beyond these practices. Do you think it's time to consider a new communication strategy or tool for your organization? Bill Gates might say it is. He predicts that social networking apps are likely to replace email.

If you are skeptical, consider a study published in November 2013 by Michael Chui, Martin Dewhurst, and Lindsay Pollak of McKinsey & Company. Here is a quote from their report:

> *[I]nternal* [social networking technology] applications have barely begun to tap their full potential, even though about two-thirds of social's estimated economic value stems from improved collaboration and communication within enterprises.

Two-thirds of the value of social media is *internal* and consists of improved collaboration and communication *within* enterprises. That's a shocker if ever I heard one!

Typically, consumer companies use social applications to market their products to customers (B2C). For an example, think of Starbucks on Facebook. Yet you've already seen that social media has much broader applications. Yammer and Chatter (Chapter 10) are helping improve communication among employees. The idea exchanges from Salesforce and

UserVoice (Chapter 3) are enhancing product and service evolution. In addition, TWiki (Chapter 5) is great at capturing, propagating, and preserving corporate knowledge. The potential of social media applications goes even further than the potential of these powerful tools.

As I write, you can build a dedicated private social network for your employees for $25 per month. (If you have more than 1,000 employees, it will cost you all of $49 per month.) Imagine this: everything that Facebook offers, tailored to your specific purpose, totally under your control. I've built five such networks and will likely build many more.

The dedicated social network construction tool this chapter will discuss is called Ning (www.Ning.com). It's the world's No. 1 service for building public or private social networks. What's more, Ning is almost like Lego bricks in its building block–like simplicity. Ning is so easy to use and valuable that there are more than one million Ning networks today.

You might wonder why you would want a private "Facebook" for your employees. You want one because it's a more efficient and effective means of connecting and communicating than the methods you're using now. Just as Gen Y has realized that Facebook is better than email for connecting with friends, Ning can be better than email for sharing information with co-workers.

Ning allows you to share information in either open or closed groups. We'll explore both external and internal Ning networks – there are compelling applications of each type. Let's start, however, with how to create a Ning network.

Start Your Own "Facebook," Totally Under Your Control

Ning provides a rich, Facebook-like set of features for the network owner. No programming is required. Instead, configuration, feature selection, layout, and design are controlled via checkboxes and drag-and-drop actions, as shown below.

Your Ning network will be available on desktop computers (via various browsers) and mobile devices. That's important because increasingly we are online using our Androids and iPhones. Here's the screen you'll see as you build your own network:

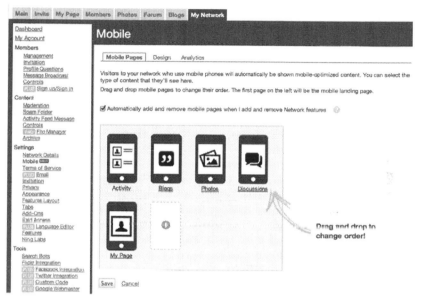

Avoid the temptation to begin by activating every possible Ning feature for your group. Unless you have a technically proficient team or audience, it's best to start small and then expand.

Conduct a small-scale pilot program with a group of enthusiastic volunteers, not draftees. Select a minimum set of features, to explore the potential communication modes (blog, forum, chat, etc.) for your group. Then assess the resulting value.

Once value is proven, expand the group of participants and add new features as users master the system.

One way to start small, with a low-risk application, is to build an external Ning network.

CONSIDER EXTERNAL APPLICATIONS OF NING

One of the first Ning networks I built was more for a hobby than a business. As someone who makes about 500 bottles of fabulous red wine a year, a friend and I built a Ning network for home winemakers. We used the technology to trade wine-making tips and techniques. We shared photos of our labels. We discussed acidity levels in grapes for hours on end.

Although I still make wine, I've been too busy speaking and consulting around the world in the last few years to actively manage the site www.CellarDwellers.ning.com, so I've taken it offline. Remember the cocktail party rule? If you're not able to participate in a dialog, then you shouldn't be at the cocktail party.

It's off topic, but if you're interested in home winemak-ing, you can still access more than six-dozen CellarDwellers' podcasts at www.talkshoe.com/tc/18. Or search iTunes' podcast directory using the keywords "home winemaking." Making wine is an awesome hobby.

Think about the archival value of this type of collabora-tive "rich media" social network. Consider how it compares to email as a potential store of corporate knowledge, especially as employees leave an organization.

At TalkShoe, we built two different external Ning net-works for our customers. One network is for the 1% of pod-casters who create content using TalkShoe (as opposed to the 99% who listen to our podcasts). We provide guidance on how to produce better podcasts and how to best promote them. The network is a win-win! Podcasters get a larger following, and TalkShoe grows commensurately.

The other network is for the even smaller percentage of people who want to build features on top of TalkShoe. We provide code samples and geeky guidance to assist in feature development. Again, it's a win-win. Users build whatever fea-tures they desire, and TalkShoe gets expanded functionality.

These days, I'm planning my next start-up, GradeNation (www.GradeNation.com). Even before I hired the first engineer, I launched a Ning network to share the concept with potential users and solicit input via a short survey. The network is helping me understand exactly what my potential customers want – *before* I start spending the big bucks on building it.

CASE STUDY: INTERNAL APPLICATIONS OF NING

Maybe you're interested in using Ning to enhance collaboration and communication within your organization. If so, start small by chartering a pilot program or selecting an individual project team within your organization.

I had great success with the latter approach, with a team of just eight members. Because the eight of us were geographically distributed, the network helped us to share and capture information. Email might have helped us to share, but email is no good at capturing information.

Our project team's Ning network name was Streakbound (an anagram of the associated customer's name). We started the project by posting countless pages of Microsoft Office documents: PowerPoint presentations, Excel spreadsheets, and Word documents. We posted all background information that would be potentially useful to team members. This was our global information repository. The information was not resident on each of our personal computers in our own quirky, hierarchical filing systems. Rather, the information was accessible securely, on the cloud, from anywhere in the world, for as long as we maintained the service.

Then, instead of sending email ideas and questions back and forth and documenting conference calls and discussions in personal notes, we posted almost everything in discussion forums and blog posts (again: accessible securely, on the cloud, from anyplace in the world, for as long as we maintained the service).

Imagine the value if a new person had joined the project team. That person could have come up to speed faster than someone who did not have access to all the project documentation. If a member had left the project team or company, that person's contribution would have been preserved even as the IT Department wiped his or her computer (including the now-useless personal files and email archive), preparing the machine for the next person.

So, to repeat the excerpt from the McKinsey & Company report:

> *[I]nternal* [social networking technology] applications have barely begun to tap their full potential, even though about two-thirds of social's estimated economic value stems from improved collaboration and communication within enterprises.

Beat your competitors to analyzing your methods of communication. What are *your* best opportunities for enhancing communication and improving collaboration? Is Ning perhaps the right tool? Don't stick with old technologies just because you are used to them.

Who Deserves the Credit?

Q: Who is most responsible for the rapid emergence of the World Wide Web?

A: There are multiple correct answers here, and Al Gore is not the best one. One top answer is Tim Berners-Lee, the British engineer and MIT computer science professor who first proposed *www* in March 1989. Berners-Lee implemented the first http connection on Christmas Day the following year.

In asking the question, however, I was thinking of Marc Andreessen. As a college student in 1993, at the University of Illinois at Urbana–Champaign, Andreessen co-wrote and launched the Mosaic web browser. In addition, as a fresh-out graduate, Andreessen cofounded Netscape with two guys named James: James Clark and James Barksdale. Marc Andreessen is one of the folks behind Ning, along with more than $100 million in venture capital. Today, Ning is part of the Glam Media conglomerate.

The question that led to the creation of Ning is this: Why would you want to have a public social network, with everybody about everything (aka Facebook), when you could have a private social network with a specific group about a specific topic? Indeed, there are applications for both Facebook and Ning. And for Google+, which is really a blend of both.

As an aside, to complete the story about who invented the World Wide Web, per Wikipedia (so it must be true): Al Gore sponsored legislation (the High-Performance Computing and Communication Act of 1991, aka the Gore Bill) that helped fund the National Center for Supercomputing Applications (NCSA) at the University of Illinois (at Urbana–Champaign), where Marc Andreessen was studying.

Andreessen says, crediting Gore's bill, "If it had been left to private industry, [the World Wide Web] wouldn't have happened, at least not until years later."

CHAPTER 17 SUMMARY

☐ Although typical social networking applications are external (mostly B2C), internal applications of social media (including Yammer and Ning) represent perhaps two-thirds of social media's estimated economic value. The results come from improving collaboration and communication within enterprises.

☐ Ning is an easy, affordable way to build a fully customized public or private social network – for employees, customers, project teams, etc.

☐ Ning not only allows participants to share information, but it captures that information in ways email cannot.

☐ By capturing and archiving information, Ning can help new employees or participants get up to speed faster than new employees without access to documentation. Ning can also preserve organizational knowledge when employees or participants depart.

SECTION 3

WINNING STRATEGIES FOR SOCIAL MEDIA

CHAPTER 18

CUSTOMER TESTIMONIALS: BOOST CREDIBILITY IN A SOCIAL WORLD

In business, we've long utilized customer testimonials to help us attract new prospects. As Chapter 11 reported, more than 75% of people trust what they hear about us from their peers. Just 17% have a high level of trust regarding what we say about ourselves. It is hard to underestimate the value of customer testimonials.

Traditionally, we've acquired testimonials in written form, but the persuasive power of written testimonials is limited. Readers know that anybody could have written or edited the testimonials. In addition, text does little to convey emotion, particularly enthusiasm.

How much better would an endorsement be if your prospects could *see* your customers talking about your products and services? Given that social is increasingly about video, we have new opportunities to increase the power of third-party testimonials. In fact, YouTube, the leading video site, long ago passed Yahoo and Bing in terms of search engine popularity. YouTube is now the second-most-popular search engine. Only Google (YouTube's owner) conducts more online searches.

YouTube makes it easy for you to make and post videos. In addition, YouTube makes it easy for your prospects to find your videos.

Unless you're looking to make a typical commercial, you don't need to hire a professional production company. A 1- or 2-minute video from a customer is easy to make and may be more powerful than a slick ad. "Slick" doesn't shout sincere.

208

HOW CAN I CAPITALIZE ON SOCIAL MEDIA
WHEN MY KID HAS TO PROGRAM MY DVR?

So grab your handheld, high-definition video camera (aka smartphone) and get out to your customers' sites. Alternately, find customers at trade shows and industry events where energy is in the air. In either case, you'll have authenticity working for you.

FOLLOW SIMPLE GUIDELINES TO PRODUCE VIDEO TESTIMONIALS

Keep in mind that people don't want to hear your customers saying how awesome you are. Instead, your prospects want to hear about what your customers have been able to achieve using your products and services. Effective marketing is not about you, it's about your customers reaching their objectives and/or serving their customers.

Once a happy customer agrees to provide a video testimonial, follow these steps:

1. Ask the person to talk for 15 seconds about the situation his or her company was in before it started doing business with you. This is the setup, or context. Typically, the person will describe the same pain that your prospects are experiencing. Feel free to guide with questions as necessary. Just keep things comfortable and conversational.

2. Ask your customer to speak for 45 seconds about what he or she has been able to achieve using your products and services. The customer will paint the beautiful bridge that you want your prospects to cross.

Because people usually talk longer than the 45 seconds, you'll likely end up with a minute or two of usable content, a great length for a customer testimonial video. No one has (or is willing to devote) the time required for something much longer than that. Further, a minute or two is enough time to communicate a few compelling points about doing business with your company.

Here are a few other tips:

- With your camera phone in hand, stand 3–4 feet away from the speaker, framing his or her head and shoulders, with the camera at eye height. This will make the viewer feel as though he or she is face-to-face with the speaker, increasing trust.

- Avoid windows and other bright backgrounds. You don't want your customers to appear as black silhouettes, as if they were in a witness- protection-program video.

- Avoid windy or noisy environments (trade shows being a notable exception). Typically, a camera's forward-facing microphone is sufficient to pick up audio that will be of decent quality. By not clipping a microphone to your subject, you're simplifying the process and increasing authenticity.

- If a particular video doesn't work out, don't worry; you've wasted only a few minutes. No rule says you have to use every take. One marketing manager told me that, in one hour, she captured 10 testimonials at a trade show. Six of those testimonies were fabulous. When this happens to you, use those six.

EDIT FOR IMPACT

To get a good video testimonial, you do not need to aim for one continuous take. Video-editing software will allow you to select just the snippets that are most compelling, with smooth transitions from clip to clip. What's more, you don't even need to learn to use the video-editing software yourself. If you know a teenager, you can outsource that part of the project. These days, video editing is a widely available skill.

CASE STUDY:
ASK YOUR CUSTOMERS TO MAKE VIDEOS FOR YOU

In a world of 175 million smartphones (the count as I write in the United States, where the population consists of just over 300 million people), almost everyone has the technology to make videos. Why not have your customers make videos for you? Countless organizations are doing just this, including many that sell B2B.

In 2009, a small winery in California decided to try this strategy. Remembering that marketing is about the customer, rather than the provider, Murphy-Goode Winery framed the opportunity as follows: Make a 60-second video of what Murphy-Goode means to you.

People participate in opportunities like this simply for the visibility that such an opportunity provides. It doesn't hurt, however, to offer an incentive. You might consider offering a few iPads in random drawings to participants who contribute during a given period. It's amazing what people will do for a shiny new Apple product.

In Murphy-Goode's case, the company offered the opportunity to become its "lifestyle correspondent" for six months at a $10,000 monthly salary. Hold off on judging whether this $60,000 was a good investment until you see the return.

Almost 2,000 people made and submitted videos. Of these, Murphy-Goode picked 50 favorites and then turned on the company website's voting capability. Not only were the participants watching each other's videos, to judge their competition, they were also promoting their videos to their friends, posting messages on all modes of social media: Come vote for me!

As a result, website traffic at Murphy-Goode increased by four times compared to typical volume. If you search for the keyword "wine" on YouTube (the second largest search engine, I say again), you may still stumble onto one of the customer testimonials made in 2009 for Murphy-Goode Winery.

Not a bad ROI for an investment that included a $60,000 salary. In addition, that $60,000 kept giving; it paid for six months of further contributions (and social media attention) by the company's contest winner–lifestyle correspondent.

I had never heard of Murphy-Goode wines before I learned of this contest. Since then, I've purchased Murphy-Goode wines many times – as, no doubt, have countless others who were influenced by the video testimonial campaign.

SHARE YOUR VIDEOS WHERE PROSPECTS WILL FIND THEM

Once you've made or solicited video testimonials from happy customers, where should you post them? I recommend putting them on your website, perhaps on a page devoted to customers' stories, and peppering the testimonials as appropriate throughout your blog. If your business sells B2C or to a relatively large business audience, you may also want to post your videos on YouTube, on your own YouTube channel.

Be sure to include relevant keywords in titles and descriptions so that people find your videos when searching for information about what you do. This alone can increase your website traffic by 10% to 20% – maybe more.

One last thought: Google and Apple are investing millions in speech-to-text conversion. It won't be long before search algorithms can search the spoken words in your videos. So include a few keywords in the content itself if you can. Your videos will only become more searchable over time.

Chapter 18 Summary

☐ Since 75% of people trust what their peers say about us (versus what we say about ourselves), customer testimonials are invaluable.

☐ A video testimonial from a customer is far more compelling and believable than a text testimonial. Plus, YouTube – probably the best-known online site for videos – is currently the second-most-popular search engine. This creates a tremendous opportunity.

☐ You don't need a professional production crew to make a video. Use your smartphone. The results are often more authentic than a slick ad.

☐ You needn't worry about getting a continuous take. Video-editing skills are widely available. Ask a teenager.

☐ With the right incentive, your customers may be happy to make videos for you.

☐ Share your videos where your prospects will find them: on your website, in your blog, and on YouTube.

☐ Google and Apple are investing millions in speech-to-text conversion, so search algorithms will soon be able to search the spoken words of your videos. A few keywords in your content will make your videos even more searchable over time.

CHAPTER 19

RSS Dashboard:
Keep on Top of Information, Without Overload

I am often asked, "What's your secret to keeping up in industries changing as fast as social media and mobile technology?" Actually, keeping up is a challenge in virtually every industry, given the exponential increase in the world's rate of change. We all need strategies to stay current.

My secret strategy is divided into three parts.

1. One-third of my secret is participating in LinkedIn groups, as discussed in Chapter 9.
2. Another third of my secret is listening to podcasts, as shared in Chapter 16.
3. The final third of my secret is using an RSS dashboard.

A dashboard service allows you to receive and organize all the information you want to receive, on a regular basis, in one platform. You subscribe to the unique collection of sources that make sense for you and then instruct these sources to deliver the information to your dashboard automatically.

There you have it – one of the most valuable tips I can offer: Use an RSS dashboard to monitor the world of mouth. A dashboard service allows you to stay organized, get the information you want quickly, and avoid overload.

Before we explore dashboards and look at samples, let's explore the world of RSS.

Understand RSS: Really Simple Syndication

RSS stands for really simple syndication, a technology that
plays a key role in social media and social networking. You've probably seen the orange RSS
button, at right, a million times on blogs, on
YouTube, in your browser, etc.

Syndication is a term obviously picked by some geeks.
I'm a geek and so is my wife. I love geeks, but in regard to the
term *syndication* in this context, I'm on a one-person degeeki-
fication campaign. I want to redefine RSS as *really simple
subscription.*

I use the term *subscription* because RSS is a lot like sub-
scribing to a magazine. Say that you enjoy reading *Time,* a
weekly publication. You could go to the store every week to
buy the next issue, or you could subscribe and have each new
issue appear automatically in your mailbox.

The same kind of process works online via RSS. As you
discover valuable blogs and other Web content, click on the
RSS button so you don't have to remember to visit the websites that provide the content you want; via RSS, that content
will come to you.

Chances are, you don't want to receive your RSS feeds
via email (although you could). You need a way to stay organized, get the information you want quickly, and avoid overload. You need a dashboard.

Using an RSS dashboard, you can display the headlines of
all your web-content subscriptions, along with the first few
lines of text. By scanning you can find the content of greatest
value, making efficient use of your time. You can even get, on
your dashboard, feeds from Google Alerts and Twitter Search.

What's more, Web content available for RSS delivery is
typically organized into micro-sliced topic groups referred to
as categories or feeds. Instead of paging through the entire
New York Times newspaper or website to find content about
start-ups, which is content I value, I can subscribe to the Start-

Ups feed, almost all of which is of value to me. No doubt, by checking the feed only, I'll miss a few random items that would have been of value, but I reduce my time with the *New York Times* by perhaps a factor of 100 while still getting most of what I need. Anything I miss will likely turn up in a search anyway.

CASE STUDY: HOW I MOVED FROM IGOOGLE TO IGHOME

In 2005, at the dawn of the social media revolution, Google created a fabulous RSS dashboard called iGoogle. You'll find a visual of my iGoogle dashboard and the other dashboards described below at http://dialogconsulting.com/dashboards/

Scan to see examples of dashboards

iGoogle was (see below, about the use of past tense) an RSS dashboard for displaying all a user's subscribed content. I set iGoogle as my home page so that, every time I opened my browser and every time I googled something, there was the dashboard. I'd glance briefly at the dashboard and, if something caught my interest, I'd click to read more.

Scan to see a big FedEx delivery mistake

One time the headline "FedEx's Apology: Expertly Delivered," from the *Church of the Customer* blog, caught my interest. Remember when the FedEx delivery person threw the flat-screen computer monitor over a customer's driveway gate? You can watch the "delivery" at www.youtube .com/watch?v=PKUDTPbDhnA.

The toss was caught on a security camera, posted on YouTube, and viewed three million times in just 48 hours (and, at the time of this writing, more than nine million times). However, FedEx quickly responded with a video apology, saying that this one incident "absolutely does not represent our 290,000 professional, dedicated team members worldwide." See the

Scan to see FedEx's apology, expertly delivered

apology at www.youtube.com/watch?v=4ESU_Pcql38 or scan the QR code.

From this example, I strengthened my own understanding of how best to handle an unhappy customer and an unfortunate incident in a world of mouth.

If you were distracted by my saying, "iGoogle was" an RSS dashboard, I appreciate that you are reading closely. In a truly customer-unfriendly move, Google terminated iGoogle on November 1, 2013. They also killed Google Reader, Google Places, and various other beloved Google products in an incredibly aggressive (but likely successful) attempt to force us to use Google+ (see Chapter 12).

Although Google+ is great, it lacks true dashboard functionality. So in one of the all-time-great examples of a company shooting itself in the foot, I used Google to google the phrase "iGoogle replacement."

Guess what? There is one, and Google took me straight to it. The replacement is called igHome (www.igHome.com), and it is an example of the free market to the rescue in that it rescued all iGoogle users after iGoogle's demise. I hope igHome makes billions. igHome offers an RSS dashboard that is functionally equivalent to iGoogle – and in some ways superior to it. You can take a look at my igHome dashboard by scanning the QR code labeled "Examples of dashboards" (above) or going to http://dialogconsulting.com/dashboards/.

I still have my favorite sources from iGoogle, but I've made some adjustments. In the center column, I placed feeds about stocks, after local weather, and in the right-hand column, I added my Twitter and Facebook streams. Among other configurable parameters, igHome even provides an option that lets me decide how many headlines to display from each source. The default was five, but I prefer three.) Every week, if not every day, I discover some valuable new RSS content to subscribe to.

If you like this automated RSS dashboard approach to monitoring and managing the information that helps you succeed in your business, I encourage you to test-drive igHome. It's a great tool in a browser on your desktop.

YOU MIGHT PREFER A MORE VISUAL RSS READER

We're in a world where an increasing number of business executives are using mobile technologies, especially tablets – e.g., the Apple iPad and Samsung Galaxy Tab, for examples. If you're one of these executives, perhaps you'll prefer an RSS dashboard that is more visual than igHome – a dashboard that provides more pictures and less text. If so, I recommend, from among hundreds, two options for consideration: Pulse Dashboard (www.ExecutivePulseSoftware.com) and Flipboard (https://flipboard.com/).

Pulse Dashboard is a snap to start. You'll be offered a variety of categories to consider (yea or nay) right on the Start screen. Select those that are most relevant to you and then tweak as you go.

LinkedIn now owns Pulse, the company that makes Pulse Dashboard and other products, so the Pulse Dashboard is likely to evolve into an ever-more-valuable business tool. Once again, you can look at a Pulse Dashboard by scanning the QR code labeled "Examples of dashboards" (above) or going to http://dialogconsulting.com/dashboards/.

Flipboard is the other RSS dashboard alternative I recommend. The Flipboard team, learning of the demise of Google Reader, posted an article titled "We've Got Your RSS Covered." You've got to love it.

Flipboard is another awesome, visually oriented RSS reader. Rather than trying to describe why not look. Once again, scan the QR code labeled "Examples of dashboards" (above) or go to http://dialogconsulting.com/dashboards/ .

Don't Miss These Blogs

If you're into technology (and who can afford not to be?), don't miss *Mashable* (http://mashable.com/), my personal favorite tech blog. *Mashable* will stay on top of technology for you, providing countless Top 10 Most Important lists and other great tech tips. Do beware of *Mashable*'s frequent video postings. The video postings are entertaining but, from a business perspective, huge time wasters.

TechCrunch (http://techcrunch.com/) and *Gizmodo* (http://gizmodo.com/) are also outstanding tech blogs.

CHAPTER 19 SUMMARY

- One way to stay current while avoiding overload in social media is to use RSS and a dashboard.

- RSS (really simple syndication or, more descriptively, really simple subscription) brings content to you automatically, as it is published, just as a magazine subscription automatically brings new editions to you.

- As you discover a valuable blog or other Web content, click on the orange RSS button so you don't have to remember to visit the site; the site's best content will come to you.

- Most RSS content is available in micro-sliced categories, or feeds. Choose only those of most value to you.

- A dashboard (e.g., igHome) allows you to receive all your subscriptions in one location. From the dashboard, you can scan titles for relevance and read the full posts only if you see they will be valuable.

- If you prefer mobile technology and/or a more visual approach, consider one of the new RSS reader apps, such as Pulse Dashboard or Flipboard.

CHAPTER 20

STOP FEARING CRITICS: USE THEM TO YOUR ADVANTAGE

World of mouth can be a scary place. For example, what happens if a former employee (specifically, the whacko nut job you just fired last month) posts a negative review on Glassdoor (the site for reviewing employers)? What happens if someone gives you a one-star review on Amazon or iTunes? What happens if someone blasts you on Yelp, TripAdvisor, or Angie's List?

We now live in a world in which reviews are everywhere. In fact, when you look up business locations on Google Maps, Google is soliciting and sharing reviews right there. We might long for the good ole days, when the *Zagat Survey* was only rating restaurants. Google now owns Zagat, which rates just about everything on a 1–30 scale.

To make matters worse, purportedly, unhappy people tell others that they are unhappy three times more often than happy people tell others that they are happy. And now unhappy people have "megaphones" to do it.

How can a company defend itself?

DON'T FORGET WHAT NOT TO DO

Don't try to manipulate the reviews deceptively. More than a handful of businesses have tried to meet the review challenge by turning to reputation-management companies to "contract for positive" (i.e., to fake) reviews. These companies are typically offshore, where the economics make this possible.

Does producing fake reviews, officially called *astroturf-ing,* sound like a good idea to you? Not only does this practice violate my PIE and authenticity rules, it is unlikely to play out well over the long term, because customers' expectations will be drastically unmet. To me, the astroturf strategy sounds like an avalanche gathering steam as it heads towards a cliff. And it is.

A *New York Times* article on September 22, 2013, ran with the headline "Give Yourself 5 Stars Online, It *Might* Cost You." Frankly, I'd be comfortable revising the headline to say "Give Yourself 5 Stars Online, It *Will* Cost You."

Astroturfing is false advertising, only worse, because it is not obviously advertising. That's the way regulators in the state of New York saw it. The *New York Times* article reported that, led by State Attorney General Eric T. Schneiderman, the regulators reached an agreement with 19 companies (this is just in New York) to stop contracting for or writing fake reviews. On the 19 companies, the regulators levied a total of $350,000 in fines. Although $350,000 may not sound like a back breaker, the financial penalty was combined with admissions of fraud. The result for the companies was rapidly plummeting ratings as the fake reviews disappeared.

Obvious suspects, including a teeth-whitening service and an adult entertainment club, were caught in the crackdown. Not-so-obvious suspects, including a dental practice and a law firm, were caught as well.

The temptation to astroturf is great because good reviews can boost business. The *New York Times* article reported that "a 2011 Harvard Business School study … found that restaurants that increased their ranking on Yelp by one star raised their revenues by 5 to 9 percent." You can only imagine the potential impact on your profits (likely a much higher percentage increase). Even so, when it comes to astroturfing, don't go there.

RESPOND TO CRITICISM PRODUCTIVELY

Don't fear criticism, and don't criticize your critics. Remember my advice about criticism in Chapter 2: Next time the talk turns negative, recognize that it is a trifecta *opportunity* for your company. Here is how to respond:

1. *Aggressively address the situation.* Try to turn it around. Remember, a customer who has a problem that is satisfactorily resolved will have a higher lifetime value to your company than a customer who has never had a problem (or at least who has never talked about it).

2. *Demonstrate responsiveness.* Even if you can't turn a problem around for a specific customer, you can show everybody else how responsive your team is. In essence, help those people understand what your products really can and can't do.

3. *Use the experience to learn.* Consider each experience of criticism an opportunity to avoid similar criticism in the future. Maybe you can make product improvements, enhance your customer support, or enable authentic reviews. Learning that leads to change leads to more happy customers in the end.

DON'T WAIT FOR CRITICS: BE PROACTIVE
ABOUT IMPROVING YOUR COMPANY'S REPUTATION

Although criticism is a trifecta opportunity, there's no reason to wait for it to make improvements to your company's reputation. If improving your company's reputation can increase revenues 5%–9%, doing it is worth some effort. But, how do you do it?

These actions can protect and enhance your business reputation:

1. Enhance products and services.
2. Improve corporate culture.

3. Evaluate customer support policies.

4. Develop an honest online-review strategy.

1. Enhance Products and Services

Think about it. If there are 10 competitors in your sector and information is flowing freely, how many are going to survive? Stated another way, if your prospective customer knew everything about you, your competitors, your products, and theirs, who would win? I believe that, in most sectors, there's room for fewer than half the players that exist today. Even among the Fortune 500, predictions indicate that, in 10 years, 40% will no longer exist.

How does your product or service rank in terms of value? There are usually just two sustainable positions with respect to value. You can be either the low-price leader (think Walmart), or the premium price–premium feature leader (think Nordstrom). If you're in between, you're Sears, K-Mart, Linens & Things, Circuit City, etc., and you're getting squeezed out. In a world of free-flowing information, it's time to race to one of the extremes.

It's hard to be the low-cost leader because you can't build customer loyalty on price. When a lower price leader emerges, customers move on. For example, it's hard to be Walmart in an age of Amazon.

Rather than struggle to be the low-cost leader, strive to be the premium provider – even as you raise prices. Here are the keys to being the premium provider:

❏ Improve products and services.

❏ Increase their longevity.

❏ Add to their competitive differentiation.

❏ Make them easier to purchase.

❏ Make them easier to implement.

❏ Make them faster to service.

❏ Lower their total cost of ownership.

Make these moves in your business before your competitors make them in theirs. Not everybody is going to survive!

2. Improve Corporate Culture

Hopefully, in Chapter 4 the story about Heifer International (2.7 stars) and Oxfam America (4.2 stars) got your attention. Perhaps it even made the hairs on your neck stand up!

Not only are employees and former employees writing about your company on Glassdoor.com, they are talking on Facebook (with 1.25 billion members), LinkedIn (with 300 million+ professionals), Twitter, Google+, etc.

Rate your company, relative to others in your industry or to companies in any industry, in regard to these criteria:

- ❐ Corporate culture
- ❐ Digital savvy (Yes, prospective employees will judge you based on your company's website, Facebook page, LinkedIn profile, and Google+ presence.)
- ❐ Hiring policies
- ❐ Business ethics
- ❐ Openness of communication
- ❐ Opportunities for professional development
- ❐ Opportunities for individual advancement (in job level or job status)
- ❐ Salaries and compensation
- ❐ Benefits (including Gen Y–favored perks, such as unpaid time off)
- ❐ Environmental practices
- ❐ Termination policies

The factors in the preceding list matter to your current and future employees. Just as important, they matter to your current and future customers. Make improvements to attract the best talent as well as to boost your reputation.

3. Evaluate Customer Support Policies

Recently I met a business owner whose company sold expensive dresses on the Internet. Unfortunately, customers often returned the dresses shortly after wearing them to one big event. Can anyone say *champagne stain?*

What is a repeatedly cheated business owner to do? This owner decided to charge a 15% restocking fee to cover the fair market value of the "rental," to say nothing of the costs of dry cleaning, processing the return, etc. To the owner, the policy seemed like a fair deal for all parties.

To avoid confusion and dissatisfaction, the 15% return policy was displayed *prominently* on the website. Unfortunately, not all expensive-dress customers read policies carefully, if at all. As a result, this earnest, honest, and open businessperson found herself on the scathing end of what were, more often than not, very unfair reviews. She had been up front about the policy. She had real costs. Some customers were acting deceitfully. But the business owner was bearing the brunt of unfair reviews.

In the age of social, every businessperson must ask "What is the cost and benefit (as measured in net profit over the long term) of a policy that is incredibly flexible and understanding?" You might call such a policy the bend-over-backwards approach. What is the cost and benefit (as measured in net profit over the long term) of a policy that might be called the refund-Nazi approach: "No refund for you!!!"? (Homage to Seinfeld's Soup Nazi.)

I don't know the generic answer. However, I do know that social media and the world of mouth have tipped the scales. People have more power than they used to have. Companies have to be a lot more tuned in and responsive than in the past.

Maybe this is why Zappos allows returns for one full year (and sometimes many more) – no questions asked.

4. Develop a Winning Online-Review Strategy

While all businesses now live and die in the world of mouth, social media has an extreme impact on the restaurant sector. This is because Yelp (www.yelp.com/), which allows customers to rate restaurants, is one of the most popular apps on the planet. Yelp is in the top 150 of the one million apps in Apple's App Store.

Using Yelp, customers rate restaurants – and, increasingly, most other consumer-facing businesses – on a one-star to five-star scale. (A rating of five stars is the best.) People can check in, write reviews, provide tips, and even add photos of the food and the facility.

Like others, I find Yelp a great resource. Because I travel all over the United States, I'm often in unfamiliar cities. When I'm ready for a good meal, I don't ask the hotel concierge or look up the local newspaper's food critic. I consult Yelp.

I'm certain I've visited more than 100 restaurants selected using Yelp. In all of those experiences, I've had a grand total of one bad meal. Because my wife's meal was fabulous (she happened to be with me on that occasion, in Las Vegas), I know my bad meal was likely an anomaly.

If you happen to be running a restaurant, you must make Yelp your ally. Unfortunately, people are more likely to "Yelp" when they're unhappy than when they're happy. So how can you protect, and even invest, in your reputation? If you are very clever, you might ask your happiest customers for help.

The Charleston Crab House – in Charleston, S.C. – printed a business card that says, "Please allow others to know about your dining experience here at the Crab House by reviewing us on … " The card lists Yelp and four other review sites.

This card is not in view in the restaurant. Rather, the Charleston Crab House has trained servers to provide this card to customers who are clearly delighted with their meals, perhaps indicating their pleasure with a compliment or a larger-than-average tip.

Remember, when people are happy, they look to reciprocate. When people receive something of value, even if intangible (say, service from your staff that is above and beyond) they will look for ways to reciprocate.

How can your team identify and motivate your happiest customers to become your advocates?

Welcome the Negative Reviews: Attract the Right Customers

Not everyone is a good customer for you. While your products and services are, no doubt, a perfect fit for some people, there are others who might not be as well served. If the latter buy from you, they will be unhappy.

The negative reviews of unhappy customers, along with lots of positive reviews, create a certain authenticity that attracts your ideal customers and repels those your company is not prepared to serve. You might remember my story, in Chapter 2, about Roku (a company selling a box to get Netflix, over Wi-Fi, to project on my TV). In that case, negative comments accelerated my purchase decision, because they helped me understand and trust the company. In addition, remember that authentic reviews can dramatically reduce product return rates. Negative reviews help potential customers sort themselves into good and bad customers. You want the good ones only.

Social media, including critics, can lead to lower costs, happier customers, and increased profitability for your business. You must embrace it!

CHAPTER 20 SUMMARY

- ☐ In a world of free-flowing information, with customer reviews everywhere, only the best companies will survive. Now is the time to address potential vulnerabilities.

- ☐ When it comes to reviews, always be authentic. Producing fake reviews, known as *astroturfing,* will cause problems. Other deceitful practices will too.

- ☐ Do not fear criticism, and do not criticize your critics. Authenticity attracts the best customers and repels the worst customers.

- ☐ Your critics (and negative information) represent a trifecta opportunity. When someone complains:
  1. Fix the problem.
  2. Demonstrate your responsiveness.
  3. Learn to avoid the situation in the future.

- ☐ Encourage your happiest customers to become your advocates by encouraging the customers to post reviews.

- ☐ Don't wait for critics. Improve your company proactively:
  1. Enhance products and services.
  2. Improve corporate culture.
  3. Evaluate customer support policies.
  4. Develop a winning review strategy.

CHAPTER 21

ANOTHER HOT NEW SERVICE: DECIDE IF THIS ONE IS FOR YOU

It seems that every month, if not every week, another hot new social media service hits the street. After Facebook came Twitter, then Pinterest, then Instagram, and now Vine, to highlight just a few. How do you decide which services to use?

In business, and even more in social, it's better to do one thing well than three things poorly. In social, the goal is not to be everywhere. The goal is to be fully engaged in the places in which you choose to participate. As such, there's no need to chase after every hot new service unless, of course, it happens to be a perfect fit with the specific demographic group(s) you're targeting.

CASE STUDY: HOW TO EVALUATE A HOT NEW SERVICE

Evaluate any service by using an external sampling tool to learn the answers to two basic questions:

1. Is the tool gaining user traction?
2. Are the people attracted by this tool in the target demographic?

To illustrate, look at a case study that shows how I guided a client to evaluate Pinterest.

Is the tool gaining user traction? Answer this question by looking at traffic stats; use Compete (www.compete.com), whose basic version is free. Below is a graph that tracks Pinterest's user traffic.

This graph shows clearly that Pinterest was indeed gaining traction in 2011, with 7.2 million unique monthly visitors. Two months later, traffic had doubled again (to 16.2 million "uniques"), and it roughly doubled again by 2014. So in this case, as in most cases, using Compete was helpful in spotting a trend.

Are the people attracted by this tool in the target demographic? To answer this question, use Alexa (www.Alexa.com), also free, to examine audience demographics. (You may have to install the Alexa toolbar to unlock this data, unless you pay for Alexa's premium service.)

In late 2011, Pinterest's demographic picture looked like this:

Audience Demographics for Pinterest.com

Relative to the general internet population how popular is pinterest.com with each audience below?

Age		Gender	
16-24		Male	
25-34		Female	
35-44			
45-54		Has Children	
55-64		Yes	
65+		No	

Education		Browsing Location	
No College		home	
Some College		school	
College		work	
Graduate School			

These charts show how Pinterest demographics compared to those of the general Internet population. With roughly 80% of the North American population now online (according to www.InternetWorldStats.com/), the Internet population is pretty close to the entire population, perhaps with a slight skew downward for the oldest and least affluent.

According to Alexa, at the end of 2011, the people using Pinterest were disproportionately females, ages 25–34, who were slightly better educated than average and a little more likely to be at work than at home or school.

Amazing? How does Alexa know this? The toolbar. Assuming that you just installed the Alexa toolbar, Alexa is now tracking *your* Internet behavior. According to the company:

> Alexa's traffic estimates are based on data from our global traffic panel, which is a sample of all Internet users. The panel consists of millions of Internet users using one of over 25,000 different browser extensions.

Alexa goes on to say this:

> Alexa's ranking methodology corrects for a large number of potential biases in our sample and calculates the ranks accordingly. We normalize based on the geographic location of site visitors. We correct for biases in the demographic distribution of site visitors. We correct for potential biases in the data collected from all the various browser extensions to better represent those types of site visitors who might not be in Alexa's measurement panel. However, biases still exist, and to the extent that our sample of users differs from the set of all Internet users, our traffic estimates may over- or under-estimate the actual traffic to any particular site.

With these sampling caveats in mind, should *you* be using Pinterest? It depends on the demographic you are targeting. If this data describes an important demographic for your business, you should consider using Pinterest. If you are a car dealer, homebuilder, or dental-plan salesperson, the women in this demographic are driving purchase decisions regarding your products or services. Chances are, Pinterest makes sense for you. If you sell women's clothing, wedding products, home décor, kitchen products, or kids' clothes, then you had better have a Pinterest page.

If you sell beer or power tools (excuse the stereotypes here), Pinterest is irrelevant for you. Spend your resources elsewhere.

CONSIDER THESE VALUABLE TOOLS

Many other services provide data similar to the two services I've mentioned here. I use SEMrush (www.SEMrush.com). In fact, I'm currently paying $69/month for SEMrush's premium offering – it's that valuable. You might also consider Quantcast (www.Quantcast.com).

If you are just getting started in social media, I highly recommend HubSpot (www.HubSpot.com). HubSpot software offers, in one platform, a complete set of tools for inbound marketing. The platform includes email, blogging, landing pages, SEO, and social. Although HubSpot can get to be pricey, it provides some of the best insights and guidance you'll get anywhere, especially when you're getting started.

As the company says on its About page:

> HubSpot all-in-one marketing software helps more than 10,000 companies in 56 countries attract leads and convert them into customers. A pioneer in inbound marketing, HubSpot aims to help its customers make marketing that people actually love.

Having used HubSpot to help clients, I can confirm that these statements are accurate.

One last point: No external sampling tool can provide data that's as accurate about your own site as your own direct measurements. To that end, I recommend installing Google Analytics (www.google.com/analytics/) to measure and understand your traffic. It's fabulous and it's free.

That said, the external sampling tools give you a view of the outside world and an apples-to-apples way to compare your traffic with that of your competitors'. That's real value.

Pause for a Reality Check: Growing an Audience Will Take Time

One reason to avoid chasing every hot new service is the fact that your resources are limited. Another reason is that attracting a following on social takes time.

Let's say you've used Compete, Alexa, or another tool to identify the best social media vehicle to reach your target audience. Even with the perfect vehicle, it will take significant calendar time – not to mention staff time, for content production – to grow your audience. Don't fall for the common misperception that growing an audience in social is quick and easy.

You might look at Starbucks' 35+ million followers and assume those followers gathered overnight. In fact, Starbucks has been posting regularly since early 2008, investing countless hours of staff time, to say nothing of Free Pastry Day coupons. Starbucks also benefited from in-store promotion and from being an early adopter of Facebook and Twitter, when, compared to today, there was relatively low competition for people's attention.

As you evaluate any hot new service, it's a good idea to revisit Chapter 7 and the 11-step process for planning your social media initiative. A lot goes into creating a successful overall program.

The fastest I've seen a social audience engage was in the case of Justice, the premium-clothing brand of Tween Brands (see Chapter 3). It took Tween Brands just three months to reach 100,000 moms because (1) the company had an incredibly compelling value proposition and (2) Tween Brands had a comprehensive promotion plan involving their 1,000+ retail outlets, their popular website, 10s of millions of direct-mail catalogs, and even Justin Bieber (a story for my next book). I've seen decidedly few companies that know as much about their customers or are as effective as Tween Brands was in engaging them.

More typical is the experience of the manufacturer of Fresh Cab natural rodent repellent, a product that I've come to love. It's effective and 100% safe for pets.

The Fresh Cab team adopted the HubSpot tool and got serious about social media in late 2011, although Fresh Cab had joined Facebook in July of 2009. Even as a small company, Fresh Cab had a full-time marketing person. This is atypical, but smart.

Fresh Cab worked hard for roughly six months, into 2012, before reaching the 1,000th Facebook Like. Was the effort worth it? Would you have thrown in the towel by then?

In Facebook, 1,000 Likes is sort of a magic number of Likes. With fewer followers, a Facebook page has no momentum. It's like rolling a snowball up a hill. The page will die without substantial and continued investment. After reaching 1,000 followers, a Facebook page comes to life with the collective energy of its audience. The contribution of the audience can exceed the contribution of the company that maintains the page.

Among other promotion initiatives, the Fresh Cab team created a business card–sized insert for product packages:

Notice that, in asking customers to Like the company on Facebook, Fresh Cab emphasized the benefits *to customers,* not to Fresh Cab. Never forget, marketing is about them, not you.

Eighteen months after this initiative, Fresh Cab's Facebook following hit 20,000 (and is still growing). The Facebook page is currently generating an impressive return on the company's substantial and sustained investment.

CHAPTER 21 SUMMARY

❒ In social, the goal is not to use every service but to be fully engaged in the places in which you choose to participate. There's no need to chase after every hot new service unless, or course, it happens to be a perfect fit with the specific demographic group(s) you're targeting.

❒ Evaluate any service by finding the answers to two basic questions:

1. Is the tool gaining user traction?

2. Are the people attracted by this tool in the target demographic?

❒ External measurement services, including Compete and Alexa, can help you answer the two basic questions about any hot new service.

❒ No external sampling tool can provide data that's as accurate about your own site as your own direct measurements. Google Analytics is the best tool to measure and understand your traffic. It's fabulous and it's free.

❒ Be sure any tool you consider adopting fits well in your overall social strategy.

❒ Once you decide where to engage, be realistic. Building a social following takes substantial staff time and calendar time. Most social initiatives require a certain critical mass. For Facebook, the magic number of followers, to achieve critical mass, is roughly 1,000.

CHAPTER 22

CONVERTING VISITORS, LIKERS, FOLLOWERS, AND READERS IS THE TRUE TEST OF SUCCESS

No doubt, you are well aware that you are in business to make money, not friends. Yet with all the hype in social media, it's easy to forget there is no guaranteed value in growing numbers of LinkedIn Company Page followers, Facebook Likes, Ning network members, or Twitter followers. As discussed in Chapter 7, you must first engage your target audience and then convert them (at least some meaningful percentage of them) to prospects, customers, advocates, etc. Engage ... then convert.

Measuring the costs and benefits of your social media programs (and more broadly, all of your digital marketing initiatives) is critical. Calculating the actual value of your programs, will give you a basis for deciding which initiatives merit increased or decreased investment going forward. Otherwise, you are just guessing and hoping. As someone once said, "Hope is not a strategy."

Consider the value of the following sequence of actions:

1. A person visits or clicks to become a follower of your LinkedIn Company Page. That person is now engaged.

2. That person clicks on your LinkedIn Careers tab, indicating a potential interest in working for your company.

3. He or she views your careers video on that LinkedIn page, better self-qualifying as a potential job candidate.

4. The person then clicks on a specific job listing, on your LinkedIn Careers page, to reach the corresponding job description landing page on your company website, further self-qualifying.

5. The person clicks on the Apply button and completes a job application.

These are five possible *conversion* steps that can lead from posting a LinkedIn Company Page to receiving a job application.

It's essential to determine your desired conversion steps, because the value of any social initiative depends on your ability to motivate the participant to execute your desired actions voluntarily.

Here is another example of how conversions from visitor to potential customer can happen.

1. A person visits or clicks to become a follower of your LinkedIn Company Page.

2. That person clicks the Products and Services button.

3. The person then notices and possibly reviews some of the 83 recommendations for that product.

4. The person clicks to read the description of a specific product.

5. Interested, the person sees and clicks on the link to your blog post about that product.

6. The person reads the blog post.

7. The person clicks on Have a Salesperson Contact Me. The person has completed the actions you desired for this potential customer.

Of course, in both examples the person taking the actions must complete an additional series of steps for him or her to become your employee or your customer. The social media initiative, however, has brought the person to the point that these steps can conceivably happen.

So much for the examples. Have you defined the conversion objectives and associated steps for your social media and digital marketing programs? For some brainstorming ideas about potential conversion actions, return to Chapter 7, specifically step 1.

Once understood and explicitly defined, your conversion steps can be tracked, measured, and even quantified. Your Marketing Team or outside agency partners should be thrilled to tackle this task because doing so will allow them to prove their value to your organization. That said, recall my counterpoint argument, also in Chapter 7: Measurement has a cost that reduces your profits.

QUANTIFY THE VALUE OF YOUR SOCIAL MEDIA

The Google Analytics (www.google.com/analytics/) free tool can track much of what happens on your website, including where people come from (e.g., LinkedIn, Twitter, Google search, etc.) and what they do after arriving at your site.

With conversion steps defined, conversion rates can be measured and improved. Let's look at a simplified example. Your reality is likely to be a bit more complicated.

Let's say you have defined the following sequence of conversion steps for readers of your blog:

1. Read a given blog post.
2. Click on a link, near the end of that post, to an associated landing page that contains details about a product or service.
3. Click on the gold Have a Salesperson Contact Me button.
4. Purchase your company's product or service.

WordPress (https://wordpress.com), your blog engine, and Google Analytics will tell you how many people read a given blog post in a given period. By tracking the number of people who read and/or comment on any given post, your team will learn which topics are most engaging to your audience, allowing your team to increase the effectiveness of posts over time.

To continue the example, assume the following:

- ☐ Your typical blog post attracts 1,000 readers during its first six months. For simplicity's sake, ignore the substantial benefits of the post's "long tail" (i.e., the fact that new site visitors will read the post after the six-month period).

- ☐ Your measurements show that 5% of people who read the blog in the first six months will execute the desired conversion action (clicking on a link), meaning that 50 out of 1,000 of readers visit the landing page you targeted.

- ☐ Of these, 10% click on the gold Have a Salesperson Contact Me button. Your Sales Team follows up as requested, making a total of five calls.[6]

- ☐ Following these five calls, one prospect ultimately buys your product or service (over the 12-month sales cycle), to produce a 20% conversion rate.

---

[6] Although the sample sizes in this example become very small and are, therefore, statistically insignificant, across *all* of your blog posts, social initiatives, and web pages, the numbers should be more statistically significant (i.e., show less variance and, therefore, be more predictive).

To summarize:

Conversion Action	Conversion Rate	Participants
Read a given blog post.	Not addressed[7]	1,000
Click on a link, near the end of the post, to an associated landing page that provides details about the relevant product or service.	5%	50 (1,000 × 0.05)
Click on the gold Have a Salesperson Contact Me button.	10%	5 (50 × 0.10)
Purchase your company's product or service.	20%	1 (5 × 0.20)

Now work backwards to calculate conversion values. Say that your average lifetime customer value for buyers of this product is $50,000 net profit.

Therefore, the value of a click on the gold Have a Salesperson Contact Me button is $10,000 ($50,000 × 20% conversion rate). Checking the math: 5 clicks × $10,000 is equal to one buyer × $50,000.

Backing up further, the value of a blog visitor clicking to your company's landing page is $1,000 ($10K × 10%). Checking the math: 50 clicks × $1,000 still equals $50,000.

---

[7] The conversion rate to blog reader is not addressed in this example. It would be derived from a measurement of the total audience to which a blog post is being promoted, relative to the 1,000 people who read that post. The measurement would include the collective costs of acquiring regular blog readers through an associated email marketing program, RSS promotion, home page clicks to the blog, etc.

And backing up one more step, the value of a blog reader is $50 ($1,000 × 5%). Again checking the math: 1,000 readers × $50 still equals $50,000.

To summarize:

Conversion Action	Conversion Rate	Participants	Per Conversion Value
Read a given blog post.	Not addressed	1,000	$50 ($50,000/ 1,000)
Click on a link, near the end of the post, to an associated landing page that provides details about the relevant product or service.	5%	50 (1,000 × 0.05)	$1,000 ($50,000/50)
Click on the gold Have a Salesperson Contact Me button.	10%	5 (50 × 0.10)	$10,000 ($50,000/5)
Purchase your company's product or service.	20%	1 (5 × 0.20)	$50,000

Now, if you're doing one such blog post per month and seeing similar results across all posts, the total value of your blogging initiative, on an annual basis, is 12 × $50,000, or $600,000. If the cost of your blogging initiative (and downstream conversion sequence, including the associated percentage of payroll for the designers building landing pages, the salespeople following leads, etc.) on an annual basis is less than $600,000, you're making a good investment. Your social marketing initiatives are yielding a positive ROI. If that ROI is better than the ROI associated with your other investment opportunities, you should invest more.

If you can acquire additional blog readers for a total cost of $49 or less, without degrading your conversion rate, you've still got a positive ROI. Invest more.

Likely, your reader acquisition cost will be dramatically different than your conversion value, either substantially higher or lower, so it will be obvious whether to invest more or to redeploy (aka reduce) your level of resources.

Note: If you can acquire additional landing page visitors for a total cost of $999 or less, without degrading your conversion rate, you've got a positive ROI and can skip a step. Invest more there.

DON'T GUESS ABOUT THE VALUE OF A CHANGE: ALWAYS BE TESTING (ABT)

You may have noticed I specified the color of the Have a Salesperson Contact Me button. The button is gold. Why? Your designer *guessed* that the color would be effective.

Should you just trust this guess? If the value of a click on that button is $10,000, your answer is probably no. It's time to test the effectiveness of various colors. Specifically, perform a *split test.*

Using any number of tools (e.g., HubSpot, http://blog.hubspot.com/, mentioned in Chapter 14), you can divide your web traffic into two halves (or three-thirds, etc.) for a test period. In this case, half your visitors reaching the target page see the gold button and the other half see a green button. All other things are identical.

During the test period, the conversion rate associated with the gold button will likely match your historical averages (10%, in this case). But if the conversion rate associated with the green version is 12% (and the downstream close rate holds true), green is the better choice, resulting in a total of six rather than five conversions. That's worth an extra $10,000 every single month.

While we're at it, why does the button say Have a Sales-person Contact Me? Again, because that was your designer's guess about what would be effective. How about using a button that says Buy Now! or perhaps *Please* Have a Salesperson Contact Me. Test your options to find out which works best.

The best way to maximize your sales and marketing profits via social media is to know your intended conversion steps, measure their effectiveness, and always be testing.

World of Mouth Is a Do-It-Yourself World

I've helped more than 50 companies develop winning social media strategies. Yet I've almost never worked with any one company for more than three months. Once a team has a compelling social media strategy and fully engages with its target audiences, team members' knowledge about their *specific* customers, market, and competitors quickly surpasses my own more *generalized* knowledge. Social media consultants have only short-term value to your organization unless they are actually running your social initiatives for you. On the other hand, why would you want the opportunities to learn and engage customers via social media to fall outside your organization?

CHAPTER 22 SUMMARY

☐ There is no guaranteed value in obtaining LinkedIn Company Page followers, Facebook Likes, Ning network members, or Twitter followers.

☐ Measuring the value of your social and digital marketing programs provides a basis for deciding which initiatives merit increased or decreased investment going forward.

☐ A visitor to your website or given social media page who ultimately becomes an employee or customer goes through a series of conversion steps, even if you have not defined those conversion steps.

☐ Understanding your conversion steps helps you measure the ROI of the associated social media investment. Estimate or calculate the value of your important conversion sequences.

☐ Always be testing (ABT) options to optimize conversion rates. Don't guess if a change would be an improvement.

☐ Invest more in the aspects of social and digital marketing that achieve an ROI that exceeds that of other investment opportunities; redeploy resources when ROI is below that.

CHAPTER 23

THE LAST WORD: THIS IS THE TIME FOR ACTION

If we know one thing for certain, it is that the rate of change in technology is accelerating exponentially. The corresponding increase of information we must master is staggering. A lot is going on out there, including an amount of content that doubles annually. This annual doubling is likely to continue for decades.

This reminds me of a quote from Jack Welch, the former CEO of GE (formerly General Electric): "If the rate of change on the outside exceeds the rate of change on the inside, the end is near."

Yes, a lot is going on out there. What is going on inside your organization? What is going on inside your head? How fast are you adapting?

If this book could convey only one point, it should be this: *In a world of accelerating change, technology is not the enemy; it's the solution.*

Technology comes in many forms. The acronyms for some of those forms are DVR, CRM, and SEO. This book is about social media, the slice of technology that helps enhance communication among your key audiences, both internal and external to your organization. These audiences include your customers and prospects, your partners and suppliers, your current and future (and sometimes even your past) employees.

The tools for communicating with such audiences evolve continuously. At one time, smoke signals and Morse code were state of the art. Later telegrams, pagers, and faxes moved to the forefront. After that, email took center stage. Now, although most business executives find it shocking, email is no longer worthy of its prominent place in business communication.

If we hope to survive and prosper, our business communications must evolve with the new, more efficient technologies. It's time to think outside the Inbox. Email looks like the telegram of our day.

The new tools are Yammer, Chatter, and Twitter. They are Facebook, TWiki, and Ning. They are even Instagram, Pinterest, and Vine. In reading this book, you have learned about more than a dozen social media – social networking tools and numerous best practices for their application. Now it's time to explore the use of these applications in your business.

Where Do You Go from Here?

If most of what you read on these pages is new to you or if you're already an expert looking to stay on the leading edge, I recommend taking one of two possible approaches as your next step, depending on whether you prefer jumping straight in or planning carefully.

Approach 1: Jump Straight into the Deep End To See How Well You Swim

Try a 3-3-3 trial: This involves 3 volunteers, for 3 hours per week, for 3 months.

☐ Start by identifying a key "communication enhancement opportunity" inside or outside your organization.

☐ Recruit three technically capable volunteers (not draftees) who are genuinely enthusiastic about attacking the initiative.

❏ Adjust workloads to allow each to dedicate 3 hours per week to working your program.

❏ Monitor their progress and, after three months, meet with the team as a group, to review the results.

❏ If the project shows promise, invest the appropriate resources to sustain and grow it. Otherwise, fail fast and try something else.

Approach 2: Craft a Strategic Plan

❏ Find an experienced expert inside or outside your organization to help craft a strategic plan, following the 11-step process described in Chapter 7.

❏ As you develop the plan, be sure to include all of the information you need to make a go or no-go decision, including information about the investment of staff hours and external dollars needed to proceed. Also be sure to determine metrics to manage and evaluate the program.

❏ After six months (six months rather than the three allocated in Approach 1, because more resources can be invested in a well-planned program), if the project shows promise, invest to sustain and grow it. Otherwise, fail fast and consider trying something else.

You might prefer a blend of these two approaches. In any case, understand your measures of success so that you can make ongoing investment decisions based on data rather than faith. It doesn't make sense to invest in social media just because everyone else is doing it.

Go Forward with Realistic Expectations

Have you ever seen the old cartoon about building a tire swing? The cartoon uses panels to show remarkable differences in how the customer explained the project, how the project leader understood it, how the business consultant described it, how the company supported it, what actually got built, and what the customer actually needed. Of course, the consultant's version is the fanciest; it's an easy chair suspended like a swing. Take a look at http://dialogconsulting.com/social-media-reality/ or by scanning the QR code below.

Scan to see cartoon
about building a tire swing

As you might guess, I'm the business consultant whose approach is characterized in the cartoon. This book has described some of the biggest successes, the "easy chair" version of social media. Your reality will likely be less cushy.

That said, more often than not, I see businesses implement the social media approach shown in a different panel: how the programmer wrote it. In this panel, the swing is a contraption that makes no sense; it has elements of a swing but is constructed in such a way that nobody could use it to swing - since the seat ends up on the ground. In a similar way, businesses create social media programs that have no practical value to the target audience; therefore, not valuable to the company.

Without outside help, you may not find yourself in the "swinging easy chair," but you can protect yourself from being the "worthless swing on the ground" if you keep the three rules in mind (especially Rule 3):

1. The Cocktail Party Rule: Conversations build relationships.
2. PIE: Use personality and keep content interesting and entertaining.
3. Pay It Forward: Provide content that is valuable to your target audience.

Your social media program will undoubtedly require significant staff time and calendar time and, possibly, some money. It's doubtful that your campaign will go viral like Tom Dixon's at Blendtec. More likely, you'll work hard to recruit your first 1,000 Facebook followers, as Fresh Cab did, before seeing much in the way of returns.

If you adopt a new application internally, you might struggle to get your culture to embrace the new tools and associated processes. Change is hard. That's why many of us are now spending more than 40% of our time working email, even as better communication options have become available.

HAVE I CONVINCED YOU?

Most people think that social media is just about marketing. I hope I've made a solid case that social media has a much broader reach. Social media is a collection of tools that have applications across every job function in your organization. That said, remember that, when you use social media for marketing, it only works if it's about them, not you.

When applied strategically, you can expect social to

- ❏ Expand your team's knowledge exponentially.
- ❏ Provide bidirectional learning, giving you double return on your efforts.

❐ Help fill your pipelines (recruiting, product innova-
    tion, revenue, and more).

❐ Help you outrun your competition.

❐ Save time and increase efficiency.

WHERE WILL YOU BE IN THE FUTURE?

In the increasingly near future, there will be two types of
companies:

1. Companies that embraced social media.
2. Companies that never tried social media. These
    companies will soon be out of business, just like
    the proverbial buggy-whip manufacturers.

In the future just beyond that, there will be two types of
companies:

1. Companies that learned to use social media strate-
    gically and effectively.
2. Companies that tried social media and did it poor-
    ly. Most of these folks will soon be out of business
    or are just limping along.

In the future just beyond that, there will be one type of
company:

> The type of company that continuously embraces
> the new social tools and technologies and adapts to
> change faster than its competitors do.

I hope this book has opened your eyes to the compelling
applications and critical benefits of social media and social
networking. Now you know there are powerful social tools
beyond the popular Facebook and Twitter services.

Use the advice and the examples in this book to identify
and implement a winning social media strategy. That way, you
can read about your organization in my next book. More

important, your company will continue not just to survive, but to prosper.

CHAPTER 23 SUMMARY

- ❏ In a world of accelerating change, technology is not the enemy; it's the solution.

- ❏ Although most business executives find it shocking, email is no longer worthy of its prominent place in business communications. If we hope to survive and prosper, our business communications must evolve with the new, more efficient technologies.

- ❏ The new tools are Yammer, Chatter, and Twitter. They are Facebook, TWiki, and Ning. They are even Instagram, Pinterest, and Vine.

- ❏ In reading this book, you have learned about more than a dozen social media–social networking tools and numerous best practices for their application. Now it's time to explore the use of these applications in your business.

ABOUT THE AUTHOR

Dave Nelsen is president of Dialog Consulting Group, a boutique consulting firm. Dialog Consulting Group specializes in helping business executives develop strategies to enhance conversations with the most important internal and external customers, using advanced social media, mobile, and Internet communication tools. Dave has more than 30 years of telecom experience and has been at the leading edge of the social media revolution since founding TalkShoe, in early 2005. He's been recognized as Entrepreneur of the Year (2000) by Ernst & Young, as CEO of the Year (2004) by the Pittsburgh Technology Council, and as Speaker of the Year (2011) by Vistage International. In his spare time, he skis the trees, runs triathlons, and makes award-winning red wine.

To book Dave:

- ❐ Visit http://dialogconsulting.com/contact/.
- ❐ Call him on his mobile phone at 412-779-2788.

CONNECT WITH DAVE

Website .... www.DialogConsulting.com

LinkedIn .... www.LinkedIn/in/DaveNelsen

Twitter .... @DaveNelsen

Blog .... http://DialogConsulting.com/social-media-for-business-blog/

Google+ .... https://plus.google.com/+DaveNelsen1/posts

Suggested Readings

Mashable (http://mashable.com), for keeping up with virtually any and all technologies.

Crush It, by Gary Vaynerchuk, for understanding what it's like to live the life of a social media CEO. (Listen to the audiobook, if possible.)

Social Media Today, the LinkedIn group, for learning along with 100,000+ social media professionals.

The Killer Angels, by Michael Shaara, for something completely different. This is my favorite book ever, an account of the Battle of Gettysburg. (Shaara sees it more or less the same way a guy named Ken Burns did.)

Steve Jobs, by Walter Isaacson. Read this book for incredible inspiration and to be grateful that you never worked for Jobs at Apple – unless you did.

Social Media Explained

Facebook   I *Like* Starbucks' Upside Down Double Caramel Macchiato – especially on Free Pastry Day

Twitter   @Starbucks luv #UDDCM on #FPD. #Awesome

Foursquare   I'm at Starbucks. Let's connect over macchiato. Just kidding, not IRL!

LinkedIn   My skills include being a morning self-starter

Instagram   My Starbucks in sepia … looks old but so hot. ;-)

Pinterest   These are my 239 favorite Starbucks locations.

YouTube   My barista making my coffee (87 seconds).

Vine   My barista making my coffee (6 seconds).

Google+   Already posted @Starbucks on Facebook, Twitter, FourSquare, etc.; hate to on G+ too will but for SEO.

Yammer   [From smartphone] At Starbucks in 10 min. Co-workers – let's meet up and strategize.

Ning   [From desktop] At Starbucks in 10 min. Co-workers – let's meet up and strategize. Here's my PPT.

Snapchat   At Starbucks on break. Glad my boss won't know … 3, 2, 1, poof!

This take on social media was inspired by @mthwgeek (there's nothing ever totally new under the sun). A million thanks!